Food Safety 101
KISS
Keep It Safely Simple

The Common Sense Approach to Food Safety

Ann Anders
REHS, CP-FS, CFSM, CPFM, CHM

Edward H. Manley
MCFE, CHM, CPFM, Editor

D1615966

Custom Publishing

New York   Boston   San Francisco
London   Toronto   Sydney   Tokyo   Singapore   Madrid
Mexico City   Munich   Paris   Cape Town   Hong Kong   Montreal

This book is dedicated to (in alphabetical order):
Cathreen, Dennis, Elme, Frandy, Harold, Lito, Neptali, Ringo,
and Shield, for it is their desire and thirst for knowledge
that inspired me to see the simplicity of what we do
and express it in a straightforward manner.

Welcome!

Hello and welcome to my second book. My most recent adventure has inspired me to write this NO-Nonsense guide to food safety certification. Yes, yes I know there are a multitude of books on food safety. So you are probably wondering, "Why another one?" Let me explain.

At the time of writing this I am working overseas on a government installation training a third-world culture, the local food service employees, on food safety. The goal is to certify a group as Persons in Charge. This has been one of my most challenging tasks since there was a HUGE language barrier.

I learned to break this whole food safety arena down to its most fundamental basis without all the "fluff" that those in the academic world and food industry organizations have added... nothing wrong with that, but "more" isn't always better. Now days, with everyone suffering from information overload, "simple" is easier to assimilate... Like Sgt. Friday always said, "Just the facts, ma'am, just the facts."

Just how many pages does it take to say the temperature danger zone is the range between 41°F - 135°F? Seems to me I just did it in one sentence....duh. Heck, let's even drop all those Celsius numbers since this book is primarily written for distribution in the United States. The less extraneous stuff my eyes have to look at, the less my brain has to attempt to process. I by no means want to diminish the fact that food safety is VITALLY important! I believe that this point can be made with fewer words.

The challenge is to get the most crucial operational points across simply and succinctly.

A technical note, I used a technique called "information mapping" which "chunks" information together. This book won't "read" like a normal book; it is more of an outline, and some charts and examples with a few transition paragraphs are thrown in.

The FDA Food Code is, as we know, the "model" for food safety. Most states have adopted it in its entirety while a few other states have used the bulk of it and tweaked certain parts to fit their unique situations. It is my opinion that every operator should be well versed in the Code. I also believe that a person who is certified should also know the Code well. Given that it is over 600 pages of rather "dry" material, most books on food safety have extrapolated the most important information. I have done the same thing.

Let's get started...

Ann Anders

The Importance of Food Safety

Generally speaking, consumers are more informed today than ever before. In the past four years various outbreaks have occurred on large cruise ships, in hotels, and other large tourist sites due to contaminated products and cross contamination from infected people. These have made newspaper, TV and internet headlines and caused the temporary closure of some facilities, and even put some out of business. The public expects and deserves to have safe food!

The following are findings from a study published in 2000 by the Centers for Disease Control (CDC) indicating that each year foodborne illnesses cause:

- **76,000,000** illnesses

- **325,000** hospitalizations

- **5,000** deaths

It is probably safe to conclude that those numbers have risen over the last few years.

Depending on which resource you read, there are anywhere between 40,000 and 60,000 lawsuits filed in the last few years with millions of dollars paid out to the winners of those cases. So, not only are your customers at risk, your business and livelihood could also be at risk should you be sued or shut down by the health department for not following safe food handling practices.

The President's Council on Food Safety says:

"While every player in the flow of food from farm to table (consumer) has some degree of responsibility for food safety, you are usually the last line of defense before food reaches the consumer. Because of this, you have a significant share of the responsibility for ensuring safe food."

The President's Council on Food Safety says:

"While every player in the flow of food from farm to table (consumer) has some degree of responsibility for food safety, you are usually the last line of defense before food reaches the consumer. Because of this, you have a significant share of the responsibility for ensuring safe food."

Table of Contents

Management & Personnel

Management:

Why Training for Persons in Charge?

Individuals who are placed in charge of a food establishment must be certified that their knowledge level of food safety is sufficient to follow food safety practices and to prevent food-borne illness.

The Food & Drug Administration (FDA) publishes the Food Code. It is a set of uniform standards for food safety. The Food Code states that:

1. There must be a designated Person in Charge (PIC) present during all hours of operation.

2. The PIC must demonstrate various areas of knowledge

3. The PIC must be certified.

Included in the duties of the Person in Charge are ensuring that the regulations are followed and that all employees:

- Clean their hands
- Check foods at receipt to determine that it is delivered at the required temperatures and protected from contamination
- Cook and cool potentially hazardous foods properly
- Sanitize multi-use equipment and utensils after cleaning and before reuse
- Prevent cross contamination
- Cease operation immediately in the event of fire, storm, flood, mechanical breakdown, extended power outage (greater than 2 hours), loss of drinking water (potable source), backup of sewage, imminent health hazard, or similar event that may—

  Result in the contamination of food.

  Prevent PHF from being held at required temperatures.

  Prevent proper, uninterrupted cooking, reheating, or cooling of PHF.

The Food Code can be found online at
http://www.cfsan.fda.gov/~dms/. In the remainder of the text
I will simply refer to it as the Code. This book will not include
an extensive glossary. If there are terms you are not familiar
with, they can be found in Chapter 1 of the Code.

This book is the compilation of the major knowledge areas that
PIC must know to become certified. Consequently, there is the
assumption that you already have experience and some training in food safety.

The Code lists seventeen items for areas of knowledge with
which a PIC has to be familiar. The next page condenses and
paraphrases twelve of those areas.

Management & Personnel

PIC Areas of Knowledge:

■ Identify how the personal hygiene of food handlers can prevent foodborne disease.

■ Describe actions that a PIC has to take to prevent the transmission of foodborne disease by a sick food employee.

■ Describe the symptoms associated with the diseases that are transmissible through food.

■ Explain the significance of the relationship between maintaining the time and temperature of potentially hazardous food (PHF) and the prevention of foodborne illness.

■ Explain the hazards involved in the consumption of raw or undercooked meat, poultry, eggs, and fish.

■ State the required **food temperatures and times** for safe *cooking, refrigerated storage, hot holding, cooling,* and *re-heating* of PHFs.

■ Describe how to prevent foodborne illness by the management and control of the following:

   (a) Cross contamination.
   (b) Hand contact with ready-to-eat foods.
   (c) Handwashing.
   (d) Maintaining the food establishment in a clean condition and in good repair.

■ Explain correct procedures for cleaning and sanitizing utensils and food-contact surfaces of equipment.

■ Identify poisonous or toxic materials in the food establishment and the procedures necessary to ensure that they are safely stored, dispensed, used, and disposed of according to law.

■ Identify critical control points (CCPs) in the operation that, when not controlled, may contribute to the transmission of foodborne illness, and explain steps needed to ensure that the points are controlled.

■ Identify major food allergens and what symptoms they may produce.

■ Identify the water source and how to protect it from contamination from backflow or cross connection.

Personnel:

Management & Personnel

I. Personal Health

Maintaining good employee health is crucial to keeping food safe. Chapter 2 in the Code covers employee health in great detail and I would advise reading it and being familiar with the information. Annex 3 in the Code provides tables covering restrictions and exclusions.

Briefly, what you need to know is the five diseases below are easily transferable to food and ***must be reported*** to the person in charge:

- *Salmonella*
- *E. coli 0157:H7*
- *Shigella spp.*
- Hepatitis A virus
- Norovirus
- (*spp. = species)

Personnel ***cannot work*** if they have had these diseases within the time frame noted:

- Norovirus — 48 hours
- Hepatitis A virus — 30 days
- *Shigella spp.* — 3 days
- *Salmonella* — 14 days
- *Escherichia coli** — 3 days (*E. coli 0157:H7)

Doctors and Health Departments are well aware of these requirements and should notify operators if the person is a food worker.

Food workers must also report any of the following symptoms:

- Vomiting
- Coughing
- Jaundice
- Diarrhea
- Sneezing
- A lesion or wound
- Sore throat w/fever
- Runny nose
- containing pus that is open and draining

In the event a food worker has been exposed to any of the above, he or she may be:

- Excluded from work
- Restricted to activities that do not involve contact with food
- Excluded/restricted from handling food or having contact with clean equipment, utensils, linens or single service items

Management & Personnel

II. Personal Cleanliness & Hygiene

This area covers proper handwashing, fingernail maintenance, jewelry, clothing, hair restraints and preventing contamination.

Good personal hygiene is critical for preventing food contamination. The Code specifies how, when and where hands should be washed.

III. Proper Handwashing

Hand washing is absolutely critical to safe food handling! Food handlers must know **HOW, WHEN** and **WHERE** to wash their hands. The washing process should take 20 seconds.

HOW:

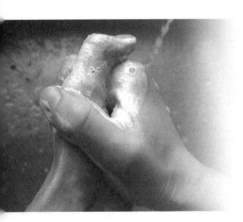

- Rinse under warm water
- Apply soap
- Rub vigorously
- Rinse under warm water
- Dry with disposable paper towels
  (Note: "common use" towels are NOT allowed.)
- To avoid recontaminating hands, use paper towel to turn off faucet and open door.

WHEN:

BEFORE:
- Beginning work
- Returning to work station
- Preparing food
- Putting on gloves

DURING:
- Food prep as often as necessary to remove soil and contaminants
- Food prep as often as necessary to avoid cross contamination
- Food prep when switching from prepared raw food to ready-to-eat food

Management & Personnel

AFTER:
- Touching human body parts, other than clean hands
- Using the toilet
- Coughing, sneezing, or using a tissue/handkerchief
- Eating, drinking, smoking
- Engaging in any activities that may contaminate hands such as:
    - Wiping counters or tables
    - Picking up dropped items
    - Taking out the trash
    - Handling chemicals

WHERE: A designated "hand sink".

Every sink must have:
- Running warm water
- Soap dispenser
- Disposable paper towels
  (Note: "common use" towels are NOT allowed.)

Workers must **NOT** clean their hands in a sink used for:
- Food preparation
- Dishwashing, utensil washing, or pot and pan washing
- Mop sinks

IV. Personal Habits and Clothing

- Keep fingernails trimmed, filed and well maintained
- Unless wearing gloves, fingernail polish or artificial nails are not allowed.
- Except for a plain ring such as a wedding band, jewelry should not be worn while preparing food
- Bandage cuts and cover bandages
- Wear hats, hair covering, and beard restraints to keep hair from falling in food.

Keep uniform clean:

- Do not wipe hands or utensils on uniform or apron
- Change your apron any time that it becomes soiled

Aprons:

- Do not dry or wipe hands on apron
- Remove aprons before going to the restroom or on break

Management & Personnel

Prevent Contamination

To avoid cross contamination, food workers cannot eat, drink or smoke in any area where food, clean equipment or utensils, linens, etc. are present.

Personal beverages: The Code states that a food employee "may drink from a closed beverage container if the container is handled to prevent contamination of" the following:

- Employee's hands
- The container
- Exposed food, clean equipment, utensils, and linens; and unwrapped single-service and single-use articles.

Disposable Gloves

According to the Code, gloves are required when working with RTE foods. Don't be lulled into a sense of false security while wearing gloves. You must change gloves whenever you change tasks, making sure to wash your hands before donning another pair of gloves.

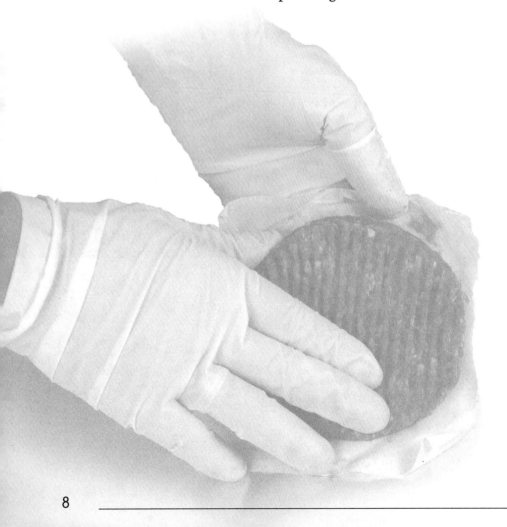

Managing Food Safety, Overview

Foodborne Illness

Very simply put — **Foodborne illness is caused by eating a contaminated food!**

In a study done by the CDC, they established broad categories termed by the FDA as "foodborne illness risk factors"

- Food from Unsafe Sources
- Inadequate Cooking
- Improper Holding Temperatures
- Contaminated Equipment
- Poor Personal Hygiene

Preventing Foodborne Illness

So if the major factors that cause foodborne illness are

- Time and temperature abuse
- Cross contamination
- Improper cleaning and sanitizing
- Poor personal hygiene practices

Then it would make sense that the way to prevent foodborne illnesses are:

- Control time and temperature
- Avoid cross contamination
- Practice proper cleaning and sanitizing procedures
- Practice proper hygiene techniques

Managing Food Safety, Overview

Foodborne Disease outbreak

A Foodborne Disease Outbreak is the occurrence of two or more cases of a similar illness resulting from the ingestion of a common food. Any suspected outbreak should be reported to your local health department or food safety authority.

Highly Susceptible Populations

People who are classified as highly susceptible are a major source of concern because foodborne illness can cause severe reactions, even death for people in these categories:

- Pregnant
- The elderly
- Very young children
- People with weak immune systems due to diseases or medications

Sources of Contamination

Contamination is the inadvertent presence of harmful substances in food that can cause illness or injury to people who eat the affected food.

Contamination can occur at a variety of points during the flow of food from the farm to the consumer.

Contaminants are EVERYWHERE and can include:

- Soil, water, air
- Humans
- Contact surfaces
- Plants and animals
- Packing/shipping materials
- Ingredients

Contamination is not always immediately or readily apparent. Many types of food contamination can cause illness without changing the appearance, odor, or taste of food.

> A Foodborne Disease Outbreak is the occurrence of two or more cases of a similar illness resulting from the ingestion of a common food.

Cross Contamination

Cross contamination is the transfer of harmful organisms (germs)[*see pathogenic bacteria on page 15*] between items.

Cross contamination most commonly occurs when harmful germs from *raw* foods are transferred to cooked or ready-to-eat foods by contaminated:

- Hands / food workers
- Equipment / utensils
- Any food contact surface

Contaminants

Contaminants are hazards to food safety. These will be discussed in more detail later. The three categories of hazards are:

■ *Biological*
Microorganisms which include bacteria, viruses or parasites all of which are too small to be seen by the naked eye....microscopic.

■ *Chemicals*
Any chemical – in a food facility it could mean the sanitizers (QUAT or bleach) or other cleaning materials or pesticides. Also, the byproduct of bacteria – As bacteria deteriorate or decompose, they produce a product that is alternately referred to in various books and on tests as "chemical" or "toxin."

■ *Physical hazards*
Such as bone fragments, broken glass, metal shavings or hair, etc.

Managing Food Safety, Overview

The three categories of hazards are biological, chemical and physical.

Managing Food Safety, Overview

Flow of Food

The flow of food includes all of the steps food goes through from the time it is harvested to the time it is eaten – "farm to consumer".

Depending on your particular position in your organization, you may not have any direct contact with or participation in the purchasing element of the flow of food. However, without a doubt your role in the food flow begins when you receive it.

You may have seen the flow of food represented in either a circular diagram or in a flow chart diagram. To make it simple, after the purchasing step I describe things in four separate categories: receiving, storage, preparation and serving. You will note in my diagram I include the steps of cooking, holding, cooling and reheating under the heading of preparation.

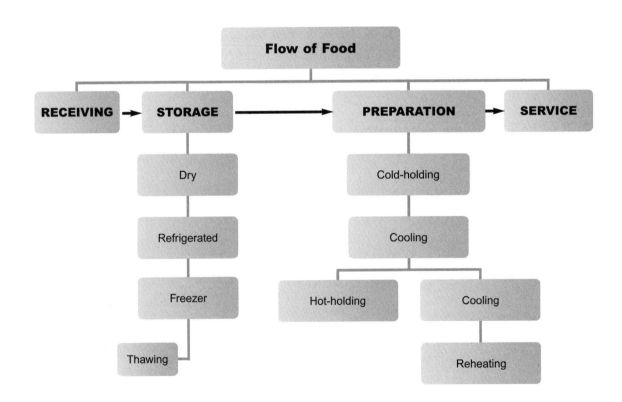

HACCP

The **Hazard Analysis Critical Control Point (HACCP)** system helps food managers identify and control potential problems **BEFORE** they happen!

To quote from our HACCP Implementation manual,

> *"It is important to note that HACCP is not a "magical" stand alone program.* **It is part of an integration of operational practices such as sanitation, employee training, and other prerequisite programs."**

> *"The key is to think of the FOOD FLOW...the path that food follows from farmer to final service to the customer. This is what you do every day...it's the things you already know how to do."*

As you follow the food flow through the facility, you are able to identify the steps (or critical control points) where food may become unsafe due to contamination, or time and temperature abuse.

Most resources tell you that it is vital to your success to conduct self-audits. In fact, certain military regulations REQUIRE weekly self-audits where the documentation is maintained for one year.

Another term you may see in the food code and other books is **Active Managerial Control** (AMC). **AMC** simply stated is where the food facility operators do everything possible to have effective sanitation and safe food practices in place to prevent foodborne illness. It is just another name for HACCP.

Managing Food Safety, Overview

Clean and Sanitary

Let's be blunt – It is vital to keep your food establishment clean and sanitary. The two most obvious benefits to a clean and sanitary environment are to eliminate:

- chances of contamination
- attraction and harborage of pests

Recognizing Food Safety Hazards

The first HACCP principle is to identify hazards. You have to identify WHAT they are and WHERE they can come from. Let's cover the general information first and then delve into the "microbiology" aspect of the more prevalent foodborne pathogens and illnesses.

Foodborne Illness:

Symptoms & Classifications

General **symptoms** of foodborne illnesses can include:

- Headache
- Nausea
- Vomiting
- Diarrhea
- Dehydration
- Abdominal pain
- Fatigue
- Fever

Foodborne illnesses are **classified** as:

■ **Infections**
  Illness caused by eating food that contains pathogenic (disease causing) organisms that grow inside the body

■ **Intoxications**
  Illness caused by eating food that contains a harmful chemical or toxin. Cooking may **NOT** destroy all toxins

Onset time

Onset time is the time it takes between eating a contaminated food and when symptoms of a foodborne illness develop.

The onset time can vary based on a few factors, the most common are:

- Age, health, and weight of the person
- Type and amount of contaminant ingested

Biological Hazards

■ **Bacteria** – Single-cell germs

Pathogenic bacteria:
- Disease causing germs
- Appearance, taste, or smell may NOT be affected making it impossible to "see" if a food has been contaminated

■ **Viruses** – Germs that live on or in other animals and humans.

■ **Parasites** – Plants or animals that live and feed in or on another plant or animal.

Key characteristics of **biological hazards**:
- Microscopic – need a microscope to see them
- Cause the most foodborne illnesses
- Prevention-based food safety programs key in on biological hazards because of the fact they do cause the most foodborne illnesses.

Chemical Hazards

Chemical hazards can be man-made or naturally occurring.

MAN-MADE	NATURAL
• Cleaning solutions	• Ciguatoxin
• Food additives	• Mycotoxin
• Pesticides	• Scombrotoxin (scombroid poisoning)
	• Shellfish toxins

Physical Hazards

Physical hazards are hard or soft foreign objects in food that can cause foodborne illness or injury:
- Glass
- Plastic
- Toothpicks
- Metal shavings (like what comes from a can opener)

Recognizing Food Safety Hazards

Recognizing Food Safety Hazards

Bacterial Growth

- Bacteria reproduce through binary fission – each cell divides to form two new cells.
- Under ideal conditions, bacteria can double every 20 minutes.

There are six conditions that allow for bacterial growth. Remember them by using the acronym

F-A-T-T-O-M.

FOOD	high in protein or carbohydrates
ACID	mildly acidic environment (pH of 4.6 – 7.0)
TEMPERATURE	between 41°F and 135°F
TIME	bacteria need about 4 hours to grow to high enough numbers to cause illness
OXYGEN	different bacteria grow at different oxygen levels
MOISTURE	disease-causing bacteria only grow in foods with a water activity (Aw) higher than .85

There are six conditions that allow for bacterial growth. Remember them by using the acronym F-A-T-T-O-M.

FOOD

Bacteria prefer foods that are high in proteins or carbohydrates such as:

  Meats
  Poultry
  Seafood
  Dairy products, cooked rice, beans, and potatoes

ACID

Bacteria grow best in a mildly acidic environment, with a pH level of 4.6 to 7.0. Most foods fall into this pH range. Some books use 4.7; I'm not sure the bacteria would notice the difference.

TEMPERATURE

Bacteria grow best between 41°F and 135°F. This temperature range is called the **temperature danger zone.**

TIME

Under ideal conditions:

- Most bacteria cells double every 20 minutes

TIME & TEMPERATURE

are the most critical factors affecting
the growth of bacteria in foods.

The two conditions you can control:

Temperature

- Refrigerate/freeze food properly   • Cook food properly

Time

- Minimize time food spends in the
temperature danger zone (TDZ)

OXYGEN

Different types of bacteria require different oxygen environments to grow.

- **Aerobic**   Need oxygen
- **Anaerobic**   Need an oxygen-free environment

MOISTURE

Disease-causing bacteria can only grow in foods that have a water activity (A_w) higher than .85.

The two conditions
you can control:
temperature and time

Recognizing Food Safety Hazards

Bacterial Growth Curve

Bacteria grow in four phases:

1. Lag phase

- Little to no growth takes place here, the bacteria are adapting
- Maintain foods at or below 41°F to prevent slipping into log phase

2. Log phase

- Rapid growth – doubling every 20 minutes
- Food safety focuses on keeping food out of this phase

3. Stationary phase

- Number of new bacteria growing is equal to the number of bacteria dying

4. Decline phase

- Bacteria die off rapidly because the nutrients have been used up and they are now being poisoned by their own toxic waste

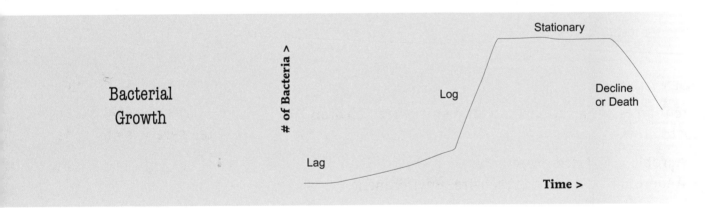

Bacterial Growth

Potentially Hazardous Foods

Potentially hazardous foods (PHFs) are:

- High in protein or carbohydrates
- High in moisture
- Low in acidity

- Fish
- Poultry
- Red Meat
- Dairy products
- Eggs
- Refried beans
- Cooked rice

Additional PHF's :

- Raw seed sprouts
- Cut melons
- Garlic in oil mixtures that are not modified in a way to inhibit the growth of disease-causing germs
- Cilantro

Ready-to-Eat Foods (RTE)

Ready-to-eat foods are foods that are edible without:

- Washing
- Cooking
- Further preparation

RTE foods include:

- Cheeses
- Luncheon meats
- Fruits
- Vegetables
- Salad items

Recognizing Food Safety Hazards

Biological Hazards

Biological hazards lead to most foodborne illnesses.

Next we will review the most common bacteria that cause foodborne illness. We will discuss:

- Classification
- Symptoms & onset times
- Common foods
- Causes
- Prevention

Campylobacter jejuni

Classification	Infection
Symptoms	Diarrhea (bloody), abdominal cramps, fever, headache
Onset	2-5 days
Common foods	• raw poultry • raw meats • raw milk • contaminated water
Causes	Cross contamination
Prevention	• Cook to proper internal temperatures • Avoid cross contamination between raw and cooked or RTE foods • Wash hands after touching raw animal foods

It is estimated that 100% of all raw poultry is infected with Campylobacter jejuni.

Cross contamination is the major cause of **Campylobacter jejuni.**

Salmonella

Salmonella is commonly found in intestinal tracts of humans and animals.

Classification	Infection
Symptoms	Diarrhea, abdominal cramps, vomiting, fever, headache, nausea
Onset	6-48 hours

Common foods
- Raw/undercooked eggs, poultry, beef, pork
- Dairy products
- Cream-filled desserts

Causes — Cross contamination – bacteria is transferred to food by contact with:
- Raw foods
- Food-contact surfaces
- Food workers

Prevention
- **Cook** to proper internal temperatures
- **Clean and sanitize** food-contact surfaces
- **Wash hands**
- Prevent cross contamination

Shigella spp.

Shigella spp. accounts for about 10% of all foodborne illnesses in the United States and is most commonly transferred by a food worker's contaminated hands.

Classification	Infection
Symptoms	Bloody diarrhea, abdominal cramps, chills, fever, dehydration
Onset	1-7 days

Common foods
- Poultry
- Raw vegetables
- Milk & Dairy products
- Ready-to-Eat salads

Causes
- Fecal contaminated water
- Food and utensils contaminated by infected workers

Prevention
- Exclude food workers from working who have been diagnosed with shigellosis
- Cook foods to proper internal temperatures
- Prevent cross contamination
- Ensure the facility has potable water for washing produce and other foods

Recognizing Food Safety Hazards

Listeria

Classification	Infection **Organism is found everywhere** **Can survive and grow slowly at temperatures below 41°F**
Symptoms	Nausea, vomiting, fever, chills, **life threatening for highly susceptible populations – Spontaneous abortion of fetus**
Onset	1-3 days
Common foods	• Ready-to-Eat deli meat • Hot dogs • Raw meats and poultry • Seafood salads • Unpasteurized milk • Raw vegetables
Causes	• Cross contamination • Improperly cooked foods
Prevention	• **Cook** foods to proper internal temperatures • Practice safe food handling procedures • Prevent cross contamination • **Practice FIFO to ensure timely use of foods**

Vibrio spp.

Classification	Infection
Symptoms	Vomiting, diarrhea, abdominal cramps, nausea, chills/fever, headache
Onset	2-48 hours
Common foods	• **Oysters** MOST COMMON • Fish • Crabs • Shrimp • Clams • Lobsters
Causes	• Cross contamination • Eating of raw and undercooked seafood
Prevention	• Buy seafood from **approved sources** • **Cook** seafood to proper temperatures • Avoid consuming raw or lightly cooked seafood

Escherichia coli (E. coli)

Classification	Infection
Symptoms	Abdominal pain, nausea, vomiting, bloody diarrhea, kidney failure, death
Onset	12-72 hours
Common foods	• Raw / undercooked ground beef • Produce
Causes	• Meat is contaminated during the slaughtering process • Infected workers not washing their hands
Prevention	• **Cook** ground meats to at least **155°F** for 15 seconds • Practice proper personal hygiene • Avoid cross contamination

Bacillus cereus

Classification	Intoxication **Associated with 2 distinct illnesses: vomiting and diarrhea**
Symptoms	Vomiting, diarrhea
Onset	6-16 hours
Common foods	**VOMITING TYPE:** **DIARRHEA TYPE:** • Rice • Meats • Pasta • Milk • Potatoes • Vegetables
Causes	Improperly cooled or hot-held foods
Prevention	• **Cook** foods to proper temperatures • **Cool** foods rapidly to 41°F or below before storage • **Hold hot** foods at 135°F or higher

Recognizing Food Safety Hazards

Staphylococcus aureus

Classification	Intoxication Can be found living in about half of the population including healthy individuals. Can grow in foods that contain high salt or high sugar and a low water activity, such as ham and luncheon meats.
Symptoms	Vomiting, acute abdominal cramps, diarrhea
Onset	2-6 hours
Common foods	• Pre-cooked, RTE foods • Vegetable & egg salads • Milk & dairy products • Foods that require extensive food preparations & handling
Causes	• Cross contamination • Saliva from talking, coughing or sneezing near food • Improper food tasting techniques • Re-contamination by poor handling practices
Prevention	• Use single-use gloves properly • Ensure infected wounds are properly covered • Proper handwashing • Proper tasting techniques • Proper temperature controls

Recognizing Food Safety Hazards

Clostridium botulinum

Classification	Intoxication **Produces a neurotoxin that affects the central nervous system – one of the deadliest toxins known to man.**
Symptoms	Headache, double vision, weakness, difficult to speak or swallow, death
Onset	12-36 hours
Common foods	• Low acidic foods • Foods packed in metal cans • Vacuum-packed foods • Garlic or onions stored in oil • Home-canned foods such as green beans
Causes	• Improperly canned food (in particular "home canned") • Reduced oxygen packaging • Temperature abused vegetables like baked potatoes
Prevention	• Purchase from **approved sources** • **Inspect** canned food for damage - Discard or refuse damaged cans

Clostridium perfringens

Classification	Intoxication
Symptoms	Abdominal pain, diarrhea
Onset	8-22 hours
Common foods	• Meat • Poultry • Vegetables • Stews / gravies • Spices • Improperly cooled foods
Causes	Improperly cooled or reheated foods
Prevention	• **Cook** foods to proper temperatures • **Cool** foods rapidly from 135°F to 70°F in 2 hours and 70°F to 41°F or below in 4 hours (total 6 hours) • **Reheat** foods to 165°F within 2 hours • **Hold hot** foods at 135°F or above

Recognizing Food Safety Hazards

Viruses Differ from Bacteria

Viruses:

- Are smaller
- Require a living host to grow

Viruses are transmitted to food by:

- Infected workers who don't wash their hands properly after using the restroom
- Shellfish harvested from polluted waters

Good personal hygiene habits and limiting bare-hand contact with RTE foods are crucial to preventing food contamination.

Hepatitis A virus and **Norovirus** are the two foodborne illnesses caused by viruses. They are very similar in the types of common foods and preventive measures. Both are primarily found in the feces of infected people.

Hepatitis A

Classification	Virus – **causes a viral infection of the liver**
Symptoms	Fever, nausea, abdominal pain, fatigue, jaundice
Onset	10-50 days

Common foods
- Raw and partially cooked shellfish
- Ready-to-eat foods
  - Deli meats
  - Produce / salads

Prevention
- **Purchase** shellfish from reputable sources
- **Cook** seafood to the proper temperature
- **Proper handwashing** and minimize bare-hand contact with RTE food
- **Exclude** employees who have been diagnosed with Hepatitis A until medically cleared

Norovirus (Norwalk Virus)

Classification	Virus
Symptoms	Abdominal pain, diarrhea, nausea, vomiting
Onset	24-48 hours

Common foods
- Ready-to-Eat foods
- Shellfish contaminated by polluted waters

Causes
- Fecal-oral route via contaminated water and foods
- Sick food handlers contaminate food

Prevention
- **Exclude** food handlers with diarrhea and vomiting from facility
- **Wash** hands thoroughly
- Keep raw and RTE foods separate during preparation, storage and display
- **Purchase** shellfish from reputable sources

Recognizing Food Safety Hazards

Parasites

Parasites are also different from bacteria and viruses. The key point to remember is that parasites are typically passed to humans through an infected host.

Parasites can infect many animals to include cows, chicken, pigs, and fish.

Parasites:
- Are small/microscopic organisms
- Need to live on or in another living organism to survive (host)
- Infect animals and are transmitted to humans
- Are a hazard to food and water

Illnesses caused by parasites discussed in this manual include:
- **Anisakiasis** • **Cyclosporiasis** • **Trichinella**

Anisakis spp.

Classification	"Worm-like"
Symptoms	Coughing Tingling in throat Abdominal pain Vomiting
Onset	1 hr – 2 weeks
Common foods	• Salmon • Cod • Haddock • Crab • Shrimp
Prevention	• **Buy** seafood from approved sources • **Cook** seafood to the proper temperature

Parasites can infect many animals including cows, chicken, pigs, and fish.

Cyclospora cayetanensis

Classification	Infection **Humans are the only known carrier of this parasite!**
Symptoms	Nausea, abdominal cramping, diarrhea, mild fever
Onset	1-7 days
Common foods	• Strawberries • Raspberries • Fresh produce • Contaminated water
Causes	• Fresh fruits and vegetables contaminated at the farm • Transmitted by infected workers or contaminated water touching foods
Prevention	• **Purchase** produce from reputable source • **Wash** berries and produce thoroughly with potable water • **Wash** hands • **Exclude** food handlers who have diarrhea

Trichinella spiralis

Classification	Roundworm
Symptoms	Abdominal pain, nausea, vomiting, diarrhea
Onset	2-28 days
Common foods	• Pork • Wild animals (bear, wild boar)
Causes	Undercooked pork products and wild game meats
Prevention	**Cook** foods to proper temperature

Recognizing Food Safety Hazards

Recognizing Food Safety Hazards

Foodborne Diseases caused by Chemical Hazards

Chemical hazards are defined as: **Toxic substances that may occur naturally or may be added during the processing of food.**

As previously mentioned there are two types of chemical hazards:

Naturally occurring – which means they are produced by a biological organism... you can think of them as biological toxins and are a natural part of the plant or animal.

- Ciguatoxin
- Scombrotoxin (also called scombroid poisoning)
- Shellfish toxins
- Mycotoxin

Some fish toxins are **systemic**, meaning the toxin is produced by the fish itself, like Pufferfish.

Some toxins are caused by microorganisms on the fish themselves.

Other toxins occur when predatory fish eat smaller fish that have eaten the toxin.

The best way to protect against fish toxins is to buy fish from an approved, reputable supplier. You should always do a through receipt inspection to make sure there has not been any temperature abuse.

Man-Made – these may be present in a food after processing.

- Cleaning solutions
- Food additives
- Pesticides
- Heavy metals (leaching metal from containers)

Ciguatoxin

Classification	Intoxication
	Ciguatoxin is heat stable and cannot be destroyed by cooking
Symptoms	• Nausea
	• Vomiting
	• Dizziness
	• Tingling in fingers, lips, or toes
	• Shortness of breath
	• Reversal of hot and cold sensations
	• Joint and muscle pain
Onset	15 min. – 24 hours
Common foods	Large predatory fish
	• Snapper • Grouper
	• Barracuda • Jack
Causes	Eating fish that have Ciguatoxin
Prevention	Purchase from an approved, reputable source

Scombrotoxin

Classification	Intoxication - Histamine poisoning
	Certain foods contain a specific protein called histidine. Histamine is produced by certain bacteria when these foods decompose. It **cannot** be destroyed by freezing, cooking, smoking or curing.
Symptoms	• Dizziness • Shortness of breath
	• Sweating • Burning sensation
	• Headache in the mouth
Onset	Within minutes
Common foods	• Tuna • Mahi-mahi
	• Bonito • Mackerel
Causes	Eating foods that contain high levels of histamine.
Prevention	• Purchase from an approved, reputable source
	• Conduct receipt inspection to make sure there has not been any temperature abuse

Recognizing Food Safety Hazards

Shellfish Toxins

Classification	Intoxication
	Shellfish eat the toxic marine algae from the water and consequently become contaminated.
	What makes this challenging is that you cannot smell or taste these toxins. **They are not destroyed by freezing or cooking.**
Symptoms	• Numbness of lips, tongue, arms, legs, and neck • Lack of muscle coordination
Onset	Within minutes
Common foods	• Mussels • Clams • Oysters • Scallops
Causes	Shellfish feed on toxic algae
Prevention	Purchase seafood from a reputable supplier

Mycotoxins

Classification	Intoxication - Foodborne illness can be caused by some types of molds, yeast, and mushrooms by producing toxic chemicals called Mycotoxins.
	Fungi are larger than bacteria and prefer foods high in sugar.
	Cooking does not destroy Mycotoxins.
Symptoms	**ACUTE** onset – hemorrhage, fluid buildup **CHRONIC** onset – cancer from small doses over time
Common foods	• Moldy grains • Peanuts • Corn & corn products • Pecans • Milk • Walnuts
Prevention	• Purchase products from a reputable supplier • Keep grains and nuts dry • Inspect foods for mold growth

Okay, about now your eyes are crossed and you are thinking, "How on earth am I going to remember all of this?"

Below is a diagram that presents a "pictorial" view of the pathogens – a "visual association." It is followed by a review of the high points.

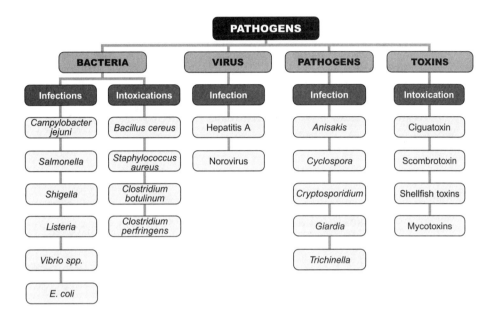

Review:

Bacterial <u>infections</u>

- *C. jejuni, Salmonella,* and *Shigella* are primarily <u>poultry</u> based food sources with similar symptoms.

- *Listeria* is found in <u>RTE</u> foods with hot dogs being highly suspect. <u>This bacteria continues to grow in cool temperatures.</u> It is life threatening to "high risk" populations, can cause spontaneous abortions.

- *Vibrio spp.* deals with <u>seafood</u> (the only one in this grouping).

- *E. coli* – while raw/rare <u>beef</u> is the common food source, it is also found in <u>raw vegetables</u>.

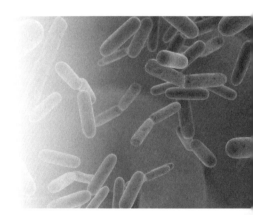

Bacterial <u>intoxications</u>

- *Bacillus cereus* has two distinctive types: <u>vomiting</u> and <u>diarrheal</u>. The more common food source for the vomiting type is rice.

Recognizing Food Safety Hazards

- <u>Staphylococcus aureus</u> – humans have this on their body.
- *C. botulinum* is the one that deals with <u>vacuum-packed foods</u>, in particular "home-canned" products.
- *C. perfringens* occurs when PHF's are <u>not properly cooled</u>.

Viral infections

- Hepatitis A is a contamination via the fecal-oral route of RTE foods with <u>shellfish</u> as a common food source. It affects the <u>liver</u> with a symptom of jaundice and onset of 2-3 weeks.
- Norovirus is also a fecal-oral contamination of <u>RTE</u> foods with a rapid onset of 24-48 hours.

Parasites

- Anisakis has seafood as it primary food source: cod, crab, haddock, salmon, and shrimp (CCHSS...this is how I remember them).
- Cyclosporiasis has berries (strawberries, raspberries) as well as contaminated water as the source of contamination.
- Cryptosporidiosis and Giardia are mostly waterborne. (not discussed in detail)
- Trichinella is found in pork and wild animal meats.

Toxins cannot be destroyed by cooking.

Toxins – *CANNOT BE DESTROYED BY COOKING*

- Ciguatoxin is associated with marine <u>algae</u> eaten by **predatory** reef fish: snapper, grouper, barracuda, and jack (SGBJ – See the Great Barracuda Jump)
- Scombrotoxin is associated with high <u>histamine</u> levels: tuna, bonito, mahi mahi and mackerel (TBMM – Tuna Boats Make Money). Also they can be remembered by the "m"s in sco<u>m</u>brotoxin & hista<u>m</u>ine.
- Shellfish toxins contaminate the filter feeding <u>shellfish</u> with toxic algae: mussels, clams, oysters, scallops.
- Mycotoxins are produced by molds, yeasts and mushrooms. Common food sources include moldy grains, corn, peanuts, and milk.

Food Allergens

Seven million (7,000,000) in the United States alone have food allergies.

Briefly defined, a food allergen is: **The body's negative reaction to a particular food protein.***

Classification	Chemicals that cause a person's immune system to overreact
	Between 5 -8% of children and 1-2% of adults have food allergies
Symptoms	• Hives • Difficulty breathing • Diarrhea • Swelling of the lips, tongue, and mouth • Vomiting • Cramps
Common foods	• Milk products • Soy products • Egg products • Tree nuts • Wheat proteins • Fish • Peanuts • Shellfish
Prevention	• The only way for a person who is allergic to a food to prevent a reaction is to avoid the food product • Avoid cross contamination • Proper labeling and warnings

The only way for a person who is allergic to a food to prevent a reaction is to avoid the food product.

* A more expanded definition is "a substance in food that causes the human immune system to produce chemicals and histamines in order to protect the body. These chemicals produce allergic symptoms that affect the respiratory system, gastrointestinal tract, skin, or cardiovascular system."

Recognizing Food Safety Hazards

Man-Made Chemicals

There are many chemicals added to foods that may pose a potential health risk. **INTENTIONALLY** added chemicals include:

- Food additives
- Food preservatives
- Pesticides/herbicides

UNINTENTIONALLY added chemicals include:

- Cleaners
- Sanitizers
- Food containers or food-contact surfaces made from inferior metals that are misused may lead to heavy metal or inferior-metal poisoning

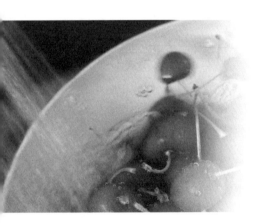

Physical Hazards

A physical hazard is an item that is not supposed to be in food.

Physical hazards commonly result from accidental contamination and poor food-handling practices.

Controls for physical hazards include:

- Wash raw fruits and vegetables thoroughly

- Inspect foods

- Practice safe food handling techniques to avoid physical hazards

Controlling Foodborne Illness

***Controlling TIME and TEMPERATURE are the most
critical ways to ensure food safety.***

Time and Temperature Abuse can happen anywhere along the
flow of food.

Preventing Temperature Abuse

Obviously, temperatures have to be monitored all along the
flow of food to prevent temperature abuse. So let's talk about
temperature taking before we get started on food flow. A non-
glass, calibrated thermometer must be used.

Thermometer Calibration

The bi-metallic stem thermometer should be calibrated:

- Before first use
- Daily
- If dropped
- If used in extreme temperatures
- When its accuracy is in question

How to Calibrate a Thermometer

1. Fill a glass with crushed ice and water
2. Submerge the thermometer stem or probe in the
   water, up to the dimple, for thirty seconds
3. Hold the calibration nut and rotate the thermometer
   head until it reads 32°F

Measure Temperatures Accurately

To accurately measure food temperatures:

- Use an approved temperature measuring device
- Locate the sensing portion (the dimple) on the device
- Ensure the device is calibrated
- Clean and sanitize the device before and after each use
- Insert the probe into the thickest part of the product
  and wait for temperature to stabilize.

Controlling Foodborne Illness

Food Flow

The flow of food actually starts on the farm where the produce is grown or the animals are raised. Two steps of the process flow, purchasing and delivery, are not discussed.

I introduced this diagram earlier and now we will go through it in a step by step format.

We will discuss the receipt and inspection of several types of foods. Then we will briefly talk about the different types of storage. Under the preparation category, we will discuss the specific critical limits that would be used in a HACCP system. Lastly we will address a couple of obvious service issues.

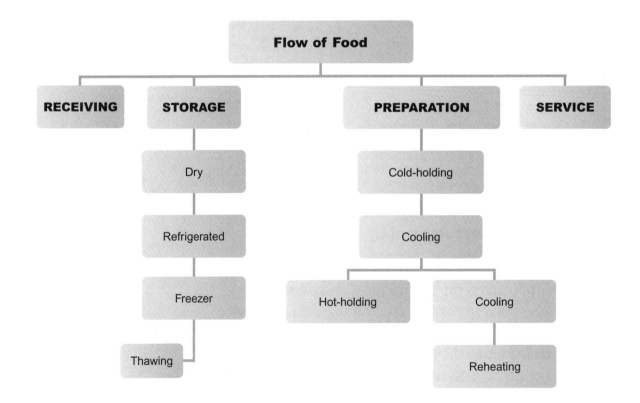

Flow of Food

Receiving: Inspection

The discussion of the Food Flow begins with the inspection process at delivery.

The first thing to do is to look, touch, smell, and sometimes taste the products to determine the quality of the food.

☑ Look at the food quality characteristics:

- Color
- Texture
- Signs of spoilage (slime/mold, etc.)
- Package (no tears/dents, etc.)

☑ Your nose knows! Smell for any "off-odors"

☑ Check the product for texture changes or abnormalities like soft or mushy when it should be firm.

Always ensure you check the temperatures before accepting. Receipt temperatures are covered in the Code and are outlined below.

Flow of Food

Receiving: Good Practices

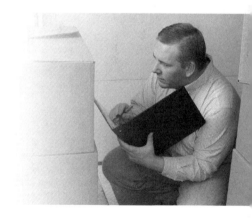

Any purchaser buys in good faith that wholesome products will show up on the receiving dock. Keep in mind food safety is the **most important** thing.

Refuse or return products that:

- Do not meet company quality guidelines
- Appear to be damaged or spoiled

A note on dry foods: Although they are not potentially hazardous foods, their packaging must be inspected for any type of damage or contamination prior to being stored at room temperature.

Controlling Foodborne Illness

Receiving: Hermetically Packaged Goods

Hermetic – **airtight** - so tightly or perfectly fitting as to exclude the passage of air; **protected from outside influence** – protected from or preventing any outside interference or influence.

Intact hermetically sealed goods are packages that are completely sealed against the entry of pathogens or chemical or physical hazards.

Common hermetically sealed containers include

- Metal cans
- Vacuum packages
- Glass jars

Check for, and refuse, hermetically sealed containers if they:

- Leak
- Bulge
- Have dents
- Have broken seals / damage around seams
- Have penetrating rust
- Have missing labels

Receiving – Milk, Eggs and Egg Products

Fluid milk must be:

- Pasteurized
- Received at or below 41°F

Whole **FRESH** eggs must be:

- Received at or below 45°F
- Clean and sound
- Free of off odors

Egg products (an egg without its shell) must be:

- Pasteurized
- Received at or below 41°F

Flow of Food

Receiving – Poultry

Fresh poultry must be:

- Received at or below 41°F
- Have the appropriate color/ no discoloration
- Flesh should be
  - Firm and elastic to the touch
  - Not sticky/slimy
- Smell fresh, no off odors

Flow of Food

Receiving – Seafood

Fish should be received at or below 41°F and have:

- Bright red, moist gills / shiny skin
- Clear, bulging eyes
- Firm flesh, elastic to the touch
- A mild pleasant odor

Molluscan shellfish (oysters, clams, and mussels) should be received at or below 41°F and have legible shellfish identification tags:

- Shells closed and unbroken
- Purchased by FDA approved sources

Shellfish identification tags (which tell where they came from) must be attached to the container until it is empty and kept on file in the facility for **90 days**. The reason for keeping the tags is in case there is a problem with, or a recall of a particular lot.

Crustaceans (fresh lobster and crabs) must be delivered alive.

Flow of Food

Receiving – Fresh Fruits and Vegetables (FFV)

- There are no temperature mandates for FFV with the exception of cut melons – they have to be received and stored at or below 41°F.

- Look for any evidence of mishandling, abuse, spoilage or degradation.

- FFV may not be normally considered potentially hazardous. However, they have been associated with foodborne illness.

Controlling Foodborne Illness

Flow of Food

Flow of Food

Storage

First-In, First-Out (FIFO) – a method of stock rotation using older food products before newer food products.

Storage principles:

- Use FIFO storage method
- Store older products in front of new products
- Store foods a minimum of 6 inches off the floor

Flow of Food

Good Practices

Do not store food, single-service items, utensils, equipment, or paper goods:

- In locker areas / dressing rooms
- In toilet rooms
- In garbage rooms
- In mechanical rooms
- Under piping
- Under water and sewage lines unless the lines are shielded to prevent leaks from reaching stored food/items
- Under open stairwells

Flow of Food

Dry Storage

The key issues with dry storage are heat and humidity (moisture).

- Room temperature should be 50°F to 70°F
- Room humidity should be 50 to 60%
- Store foods out of direct sunlight
- Store foods 6 inches off the floor

Flow of Food

Refrigeration

Controlling Foodborne Illness

Refrigeration can slow bacteria growth.

- Keep refrigerator in good repair and ensure a thermometer is located in the warmest part (such as close to the door) to help with monitoring the temperature
- Store potentially hazardous foods at or below 41°F
- Don't overload, stack items so that the cold air can circulate around them and cool the products
- Use open shelving – don't line the shelves with any thing such as aluminum foil, which prevents the air from circulating
- Never place large quantities of HOT foods directly into the refrigerator – use proper cooling techniques as described on page 46
- Store raw products <u>under</u> cooked and ready-to-eat foods
- Store species of animals in the following order from top to bottom:
  - Cooked and ready-to-eat foods
  - Fish and other red meats
  - Ground beef and ground pork
  - Poultry and eggs

Flow of Food

Freezers

Freezers:

- Keep foods frozen
- Keep freezer in good repair and ensure a thermometer is located in the warmest part to help with monitoring the temperature
- Hold foods at or below 0°F
- Don't overload, stack items so that the cold air can circulate around them and cool the products

Controlling Foodborne Illness

Flow of Food

Thawing

Thawing methods:

- **In a refrigerator**

    PREFERRED – as it keeps food out of the temperature danger zone

- **In a microwave**

    Must be part of a continuous cooking process

- **Completely submerged in cool (≤ 70°F), potable running water**

    Clean and sanitize the sink prior to use

- **As part of the cooking process**

    i.e. frozen hamburgers on the grill

NEVER THAW FOODS AT ROOM TEMPERATURE!

Flow of Food

Cooking

Cooking ensures the destruction of foodborne pathogens commonly found in some foods. Food facilities that choose to serve certain foods raw increase their risk of causing a foodborne illness. Make sure that a Consumer's Advisory is posted.

Cooking decreases the risk of foodborne illness.

- There is a relationship between time and temperature for cooking certain types of food as noted below (poultry, ground beef, etc.)
- Requirements for cooking should include:
  - Required final temperature
  - Amount of time it must be cooked at that temperature

Flow of Food

Cooking – Minimum Temperature and Time Requirements

To reduce or destroy foodborne illness pathogens, certain PHF must be heated to specific minimum temperatures for a minimum amount of time.

Poultry, Stuffed Meats
165°F for 15 sec.

    Ground Beef and Pork
    155°F for 15 sec.

        Eggs, Beef/Pork, Fish
        145°F for 15 sec.

            Beef Roast (medium), Pork Roast, Ham
            145°F for 15 sec.

                Beef Roast (rare), Pork Roast
                130°F for 112 minutes

If a dish contains more than one of the above items, it must be cooked to the highest temperature.

Controlling Foodborne Illness

Controlling Foodborne Illness

Cooling

Cooling is the act of reducing the temperature of properly cooked food to 41°F or below.

This is probably the area that gets facilities into the most trouble... cooling hot foods too slowly. When it comes to temperature abuse, improper cooling is the most common cause of foodborne illness.

After proper cooking, PHFs not used for immediate service or hot holding should be cooled:

↓ **from 135°F to 70°F in 2 hours.**

↓ **then from 70°F to 41°F in 4 hours.**

= Total cooling time of 6 hours

PHFs must be cooled to 41°F or below in four hours or less if prepared from ingredients at room temperature, such as reconstituted food (like powdered milk) and canned tuna. Refrigerating the tuna prior to preparation helps reduce the cooling time.

Rapid cooling can be achieved by:

- Using shallow pans 3" or less
- Separating into smaller/thinner portions
- Using blast chillers
- Stirring while cooling
- Ice wands
- Using ice baths
- Using stainless steel pans to facilitate heat transfer

Flow of Food

Reheating

All PHFs that are cooked and then cooled must be reheated for hot holding to at least **165°F** for 15 seconds. The reheating must be done rapidly and cannot exceed 2 hours.

Flow of Food

Cold-Holding & Hot-Holding

Hot-holding: Maintaining the internal temperature of the food at or above **135°F**.

Cold-holding: Maintaining the internal temperature of the food at or below **41°F**.

Flow of Food

Service – Food Handling

Good food handling practices help keep food safe:

- Frequent hand washing and good personal hygiene
- No bare hand contact with ready-to-eat foods
- Handle utensils correctly
- "In use" utensils should be positioned so that handles don't touch the food

Flow of Food

Service – Self-Service Bars

Self-service bars can be hot or cold-holding.

> **Maintain hot foods ≥ 135°F**
> **Maintain cold foods ≤ 41°F**

Self-service bars:

- Must have sneeze guards
- Ensure customers get a clean plate or bowl when returning for additional food
- Must have trained personnel who monitor temperatures

Controlling Foodborne Illness

Facilities, Equipment & Utensils

Chapters 4, 5, and 6 in the **Code** cover these areas separately. This section is the compiled and condensed information.

Facilities

While we are primarily concerned about the food safety aspect of a facility, keep in mind that all facilities have to meet all zoning, building and fire codes.

Specifically in food preparation areas, the *walls, floors* and *ceilings* are to be:

- Smooth (impervious – meaning nowhere for the bacteria to hide)
- Durable
- Easily cleanable
- Floor and wall juncture (seam) is to be coved and sealed.
- Carpeting is **NOT** allowed.

Lighting has to have a protective shielding. That can be in the form of a light cover or shatter-resistant coated bulbs.

There are minimum lighting intensity requirements. Lighting is measured by "foot candles," which is a common unit of measurement used to calculate adequate lighting levels of workspaces.

- **10 foot candles** – Walk-in refrigerators and dry storage
- **20 foot candles** – Consumer self service areas, reach-in and under-counter refrigerators
- **50 foot candles** – Surfaces where food workers are working with food or with utensils or equipment such as knives, slicers, grinders or saws where employee safety is a factor.

Ventilation is necessary to keeps rooms free of excessive heat, steam, condensation, vapors, obnoxious odors, smoke, and fumes. Hoods have to be made from stainless steel and prevent grease from dripping back onto food. Filters must be removable for easy cleaning.

Facilities, Equipment & Utensils

Handwashing sinks shall

- Be conveniently located in food preparation and dispensing, dish and pot washing areas, and in or immediately adjacent to toilet rooms
- Provide water at a temperature of at least 100°F through a mixing valve or combination faucet
- Be accessible at all times for employee use – in other words, access to the sink CANNOT be blocked by other items, such as mop buckets, carts, etc.
- **NOT** be used for any purpose other than hand washing

Equipment and Utensils

The **Code** specifies the characteristics of materials used in the construction of utensils and food contact equipment to be:

- Durable
- Corrosion-resistant
- Nonabsorbent
- Have a smooth easily cleanable surface
- Resistant to pitting, chipping, scratching, etc.

Stainless steel is the preferred material. There are very specific limitations on the use of certain materials like cast iron, lead, copper, galvanized metal, and wood.

A cast iron surface can be used for cooking and serving if the process is uninterrupted from cooking to serving.

A hard maple, close-grained wood can be used for cutting boards, cutting blocks, bakers' tables, rolling pins, salad bowls and chopsticks.

All food service equipment and utensils must be certified by NSF or Underwriters Laboratories (UL), and must be calibrated at regular interval."

Preventive Maintenance

Failure to have a comprehensive PM program in place can lead to biological (hiding in cracks), chemical (oil drips) and physical (bolts falling off) hazards into your food. The same would be true if your suppliers didn't have a PM program in place, thus, be sure they do.

Facilities, Equipment & Utensils

Dishwashing Equipment:

Cleaning and **sanitizing** equipment and utensils are some of the most important tasks in any food facility (more detail on cleaning and sanitizing in the next chapter).

An important key to proper dishwashing is that it helps to prevent cross contamination.

Manual Washing:

The manual dishwashing process is performed in a three-compartment sink:

- "Sink compartments shall be large enough to accommodate the largest equipment and utensils"
- Adequate drainboards to allow equipment and utensils to air-dry properly

A three-compartment sink set up:

- **Compartment 1: Wash** in a detergent solution with water of 110°F or as specified by detergent manufacturer
- **Compartment 2: Rinse** with water of 120°F
- **Compartment 3: Sanitize** using the hot water or chemical method

Two acceptable methods for sanitizing are:

- **Hot-water method**—maintained at **171°F** or above
- **Chemical method**—must have test kit available

Chemical	Concentration (ppm)*	Water temperature
Chlorine**	50ppm	75°F
Iodine	12.5-25ppm	75°F
Quat***	100-200ppm****	75°F

*Parts per million
**Without consideration of water pH
***Affected by water hardness
****Or as indicated by manufacturer's directions

Mechanical Washing:

The mechanical methods with machines are a little easier to manage because the machine cycles do processes automatically. With that said, not all machines are the same.

There are stationary rack machines and conveyor machines. The wash water temperatures vary from machine to machine with ranges from 150°F to 165°F.

Remember, these are the temperatures as they leave the manifold (the water spray arm) on the machine. The water temperature is a little lower by the time it hits the items going through the machine.

For the sanitizing cycle, the hot water has to be at least 180°F for all machines except the stationary rack, single temperature machine which is 165°F when it reaches the item being sanitized.

The dishwashing *process* differs very little for each of the methods.

They both include:

- Pre-rinsing
- Wash
- Rinse
- Sanitize
- Air-dry
- Store properly

The mechanical method includes the "racking" of the items going through the machine.

Cleaning & Sanitizing

The cleaning and sanitizing aspects of the Code are spread throughout the chapters, not isolated in one chapter.

Cleaning is removing soil and food particles from equipment and utensils.

Sanitizing is reducing the number of harmful germs to a safe level.

Cleaning is straight forward – you scrub it until you don't see soil or food debris. That includes using the right detergent to get rid of the different types of soil and food, making sure the water temperatures are correct. Depending on what part of the country a person is located in, quality of the water, such as hardness, can affect the cleaning process.

The surface has to be clean before it can be sanitized!

Sanitizing requires applying either a chemical sanitizer or hot water long enough to kill pathogenic (disease causing) germs that we cannot see.

Remember that sanitizing can be done either by a chemical method or a **heat/hot** water method. The temperature and chemical concentrations are listed on page 50.

The heat method is simple and easily monitored by taking the temperature of the water or recording the gauge on a machine.

Chemicals are affected by several other factors. They are weakened as they work and become diluted or contaminated. They have to be monitored for concentration strength and replaced when the levels drop below guidelines. As noted on page 50, chlorine can be affected by the pH of the water, while Quats are affected by water hardness.

VERY IMPORTANT: Wiping cloths must be kept in the sanitizer solution when not in use. They don't belong "tucked" under your belt or apron tie or thrown over your shoulder.

How Often?

If you become that proverbial "fly on the wall" you can see that some form of cleaning/sanitizing is happening a good portion of the time the facility is operating.

The **Code** does specify certain instances that will be covered here.

Food contact surfaces used with potentially hazardous foods must be cleaned **every four hours** including:

- Before each use with a different type of raw animal food such as beef, fish, lamb, pork or poultry
- Each time there is a change from working with raw foods to working with ready-to-eat foods
- Between uses with raw fruits and vegetables and with potentially hazardous foods
- Before using or storing a food thermometer
- At any time during the operation when contamination may have occurred

Food contact surfaces used with non-potentially hazardous food must be cleaned:

- Any time contamination may have occurred
- At least every 24 hours for:
  - Ice tea dispensers
  - Customer self-service utensils such as tongs, ladles, scoops, etc
- Before restocking customer self-service equipment such as condiment dispensers and display containers
- At a frequency specified by the manufacturer's guide lines for equipment like ice bins, beverage dispensers coffee bean grinders, etc.

Cleaning & Sanitizing

General Cleaning

"Physical facilities shall be cleaned as often as necessary to keep them clean."

General facility surface areas have to be cleaned as well. The below areas should have a cleaning schedule:

- Floors and floor drains
- Walls
- Ceiling – lights, fans, fan grates, and light covers

The bulk of the above type of cleaning is to de done when the least amount of food is exposed.

OSHA Requirements

Remember any and all chemicals used in a facility can be dangerous. Employees must be protected at all times. Each chemical has a material safety data sheet (MSDS).

The Occupational Safety and Health Administration (OSHA) requires food establishments have MSDS "Right-to-Know" sheets for all chemicals used in the establishment.

The MSDS sheets must be "readily available" for all employees. All employees handling chemicals as a routine part of their job need to be properly trained on chemical hazards.

MSDS provide the following information:

- Ingredients
- Physical and chemical characteristics
- Fire, explosion, reactivity, and health hazard data
- How to handle chemicals safely
- Possible protective equipment that may be needed
- Recommended first aid procedures for exposure

Facility Management

This chapter will cover a potpourri of topics that go into over-all management of a food service facility:

Overall facility appearance
Garbage and refuse
Plumbing
Pest control

Overall Facility Appearance

When you stand across the street and look back at your facil-ity, what do you see? Most employees come in through the back door...you know, the one by the smelly dumpster! But what do your customers see?

Take a hard look at the building, the parking lots, and general landscaping. Are they clean and free of litter? Is the land-scaping tidy?

Garbage and Refuse

Plain and simple – garbage attracts pests! Needless to say, proper garbage containment and disposal are critical to pre-venting contamination of food and equipment.

Inside, make sure there are adequate numbers of trash con-tainers near working areas.

- For containers that have food residue in them, keep them covered when not in continuous use
- Line the containers with plastic bags
- Empty when full or on a regular basis
- Clean as often as necessary to prevent build up of grime

Outside

- Keep containers covered
- Clean containers frequently so as not to attract pests or provide harborage
- Keep area clean and litter free
- Ensure garbage is removed often

Facility Management

Plumbing

The plumbing codes are just about as thick as the food code. There are a few key points you need to know for your facility.

Plumbing must be installed to ensure there are no cross connections with the potable (drinkable) water system. Simply, a cross connection is where there could be a physical link to any contaminants from drains or sewer lines.

Backflow is where a reverse flow of contaminants flow back into the potable water system thereby contaminating the potable water. Generally this happens when there is a drop in water pressure causing a sucking action that pulls the contaminants into the system.

Backflow prevention can be achieved either through an air gap or backflow prevention device.

- An **air gap** is just what it sounds like. It is a "gap" between the water supply outlet device (faucet) and the top of a sink or drain or drain line. For a sink this means the faucet can't be below the level the water could rise in the sink. For something like the pipe coming out of a steamer which always goes down the side of the steamer and is positioned over a floor drain, the gap should be twice the diameter of the outlet pipe, i.e. if the pipe is 1" then the gap should be 2". However, it should never be less than 1".

- A **backflow prevention** device is usually a plumbing valve that allows only one-way flow. There are several types of valves for different circumstances. For instance as a simple example, it could be a valve device that would go between a hose and a faucet so that the water could only flow one way – out of the faucet and not back into the water supply.

A cross connection is where there could be a physical link to any contaminants from drains or sewer lines.

Pest Control

No one likes to think about "pests" in a food facility. But the reality is that operators must take very proactive measures to prevent "attracting" or "inviting" pests into the facility.

Those proactive measures are a viable pest control program. Now that doesn't mean that you keep a case of insecticide in the store room "just in case." It is the common sense things that have the most effect.

First – Just prevent them from getting in. Use air curtains, or screens on doors or windows that open to the outside. Make sure there are no holes, cracks or crevasses in walls, doors or windows. Insects and rodents can enter through the tiniest of openings.

Second – KEEP IT CLEAN! Don't attract them in the first place! Eliminate all food and water sources. Keeping products off the floor and removing cardboard and trash eliminates a harborage area as well.

Third – Use a professional, licensed pest control operator (PCO) to monitor the facility and eliminate any pests that may enter. In a commercial establishment, as the facility operator you cannot apply pesticides. A licensed PCO must be used.

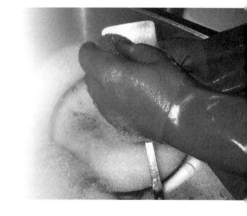

You will hear the term Integrated Pest Management (IPM) program. It is simply a system or program where the facility **eliminates** and **controls** pests. Common sense tells us that if we eliminate the pests from getting inside to begin with... the control measures will be minimal. So aim to eliminate! The above procedures aimed at elimination can be done as a matter of routine with a well trained staff.

A start to the elimination of entry is to make sure that the people who receive products are inspecting to make sure no "pests" are hitching a ride into your facility.

Another key area is to make sure the outside trash/garbage containers and the areas around them are kept clean. Keep the containers covered. Make sure there is no standing water, which attracts insects.

Facility Management

The "pests" that we are primarily talking about are flies, cockroaches, and rodents (mice & rats).

Insects

I always have to chuckle to myself when other books launch into the differences between the housefly and the blowfly or the American versus the Oriental cockroach. If there is anyone out there like me, I just smash the darn thing and get rid of it! It is really up to your pest control operator to make those determinations so he/she knows what type of product has to be used to eliminate them.

So needless to say... I'm not going to talk about the different species. You know what a fly and a cockroach look like... identifying them is not your primary concern. Both of them carry disease and as long as you practice good elimination and control practices to keep them out of your facility, they won't be a problem... regardless of what species they are.

The one thing you do have to be concerned with is if you find cockroach "casings." This could be a sign that you have an infestation. Always make sure they are swept up and discarded. As an operator, the one thing that you should know when using chemical control measures is that the chemicals kill only the live (hatched) insects. The chemicals do not affect the casings. Therefore, when the new casings hatch, you have a new population that has to be treated.

Rodents

No one likes to think they have those "critters" in their facility. They carry many disease causing germs! In addition to being down right nasty little vermin, they damage property and food products. Because of their habits, they also contaminate large amounts of food.

Suffice it to say, I am not going to discuss the different species of rodents. One tell-tale fact most people know is that rats are larger than mice. Depending on where you are located as to the habits of the local rodent population....they are actually smart and adapt to their environment. They are good climbers and contrary to popular belief, are good swimmers as well.

Facility Management

Because rodents are nocturnal, you will rarely see them in the daytime. However there are some very specific signs you can see that may indicate they are in or around your facility. Your pest control operator is trained to look for these, but you should be knowledgeable enough to know you may have a problem to bring to their attention.

Here are four common and easily apparent signs of rodents:

- **Droppings**
  - Fresh ones – shiny and black
  - Old ones – grey, dry and hard
- **Rub marks**
  - Rodents have poor eye sight; but their sense of smell, touch and hearing are very good. Consequently, they stay close to walls and their body oil and filth will create rub marks
- **Gnawing**
  - Rodent's teeth grow continuously; gnawing keeps them short enough to use and keep from killing themselves
  - If you find light colored and well defined teeth marks, the gnawing is fresh
- **Nesting**
  - Rodents build their nests of cardboard, paper, straw, insulation, pillow fillings and any assortment of things they can find

Controls

Controls are simple: prevent and control!

- Keep it clean
- Eliminate food, water and harborage areas
- Rodent proof the building by sealing all holes and cracks
- Use bait boxes (also called bait stations or mechanical box traps) particularly outside
- Glueboards usually aren't sufficient for rodents but work fairly well for insects
- Only a professional pest control operator can apply chemical pesticides or rodenticides, which should be used as a last resort
- No poisoned bait is allowed
- Schedule regular audits by your staff or a PCO so you are always on top of problems

Ed Manley
MCFE, CHM, CPFM
IFSEA Food Safety

EHMA
2609 Surfwood Drive
Las Vegas, NV 89128
Tel; 702-430-9217
Fax: 702-430-9223
ed@ehmanley.com

IFSEA Food Safety

CPFM Food Safety Manager Certification

The Certified Professional Food Manager (CPFM) is one of the three programs equally accepted by the Conference for Food Protection, and is thus accepted by all jurisdictions we are aware of that accept any of them. ServSafe and National Registry exams available on request.

Requirements:
Study the book, take a class, order an on-line training program—your choice, depending on your existing knowledge.

IFSEA HACCP Manager

HACCP is a global food safety system that covers the principles of safe food management, time/temperature requirements, foodborne illness and methods for handling and monitoring food protection procedures.

Requirements:
Where available, we recommend a physical class. Check our website for class locations.
However if:
• You have completed a food safety manager course, like CPFM, and thus have a solid knowledge of food safety
• You have the ability to grasp concepts from reading a book and completing a web-based training program

Then, order the IFSEA Food Safety HACCP package,
which includes the Study Guide, class or web-based training program, test and certificate.

"By encouraging members to be IFSEA Food Safety certified, IFSEA has been instrumental in raising the standards of the food service industry," says Ed Manley, IFSEA's Manager of IFSEA Food Safety. "That's one of the many reasons we've aligned ourselves with Prometric. They've been an industry leader in promoting HACCP, which has proven to be very timely with the incidents of food contamination nationally and worldwide in recent years."

A Valuable Resource

IFSEA Symposiums Get the Job Done

Four-day programs that encompass CPFM, HACCP and IFSEA's professional certifications are offered regularly throughout the world, including Germany, Japan, Hawaii, Alaska and throughout the continental U.S. Successful students add MCFE, CHM, CPFM to their business cards and resumes. Almost every week we hear from someone who got a job, a promotion and/or a pay raise as a result of having attended a Symposium. Dates and locations at www.ehmanley.com.

Accessible Anywhere

• Order study materials–Book, Web
• Receive study tips and E-mail help through VIPFoodSafety
• Study in groups or independently
• When ready, take the test, hard copy or, for some, on-line
• We accept government credit cards
• In some cases, VA approved for reimbursement; Dantes listing.
• Attend an IFSEA Symposium and be done in a week.

IFSEA
100+
years
FOUNDED 1901
Gold Seal
APPROVED

International Food Service Executives Association

IFSEA Certification

IFSEA Certification reflects the highest level of professionalism in your work experience and educational background.

...It says you have achieved all the necessary job skills.

...*And* gives you that critical extra special edge to stand out in today's highly competitive work place. Professionals who highlight their differences land the best jobs. Let certification make a crucial difference in YOUR career!

IFSEA has chosen to work with the American Hotel & Lodging Association, Pearson Education, Prometric, and E. H. Manley and Associates to provide premium training and testing materials, and good career advice and support to military and civilian food service professionals. Together, we preach education, certification, and preparation for a work life that has multiple career options and maximizes your potential.

Why Certification?

- **Highlights Your Experience**
- **Denotes Professionalism**
- **Shows Career Commitment**
- **Job Search Advantage**
- **Peer Prestige**
- **Personal Self-Fulfillment**
- **Use your CFM/ CFE/CPFM/ CBM on Business Cards, Resumes, etc.**
- **Military Promotions and SEI**
- **Create Points of Difference**

MCFE

Master Certified Food Executive, the highest level of the certifications, requires a 70+ on a comprehensive 200-question, 4-hour exam. A sample exam and guide are on the web site. Job security — pass this difficult test and you have PROOF that you know your craft. Certification is important today; but will be the "price of entry" for good jobs in the future.

CFE

CFE, the middle level of our certifications, requires a 70+ on a comprehensive examination which uses 80 of the less difficult CFE questions. Or, score 65–69 on the MCFE examination. Ideal for those who need more time to prepare for the 200 questions, yet want a significant certification NOW.

CFM

Certified Food Manager, the entry level to our certification program, requires a 70+ on a comprehensive examination or score 60–64 on the MCFE examination. Geared to military, students and others with less restaurant-specific knowledge who wish to be certified NOW while preparing to use the study materials and/or Symposiums to move higher.

Requirements:
Pass the MCFE, CFE or CFM test.
No forms to complete.

CBM

Certified Beverage Manager stands alone as a symbol of professionalism within the F&B management segment of the industry. In cooperation with Pearson Education, we have developed a program which teaches practical information regarding purchasing, marketing, food pairings, glassware and more. Pearson Education is one of the leading providers for content in Culinary Arts, Hospitality, and Hotel and Casino Management. Their professional relationships with associations put us in the best position to provide the materials that industry and academia alike will need.

Training Materials:
Visit the IFSEA website to order.

IFSEA Headquarters
Tel.: 800-893-5499
E-mail: hq@ifsea.com

HACCP Implementation
A Quick Reference Manual

Managing Your
Food Safety System

Ann Anders
REHS, CP-FS, CFSM, CPFM, CHM

Edward H. Manley
MCFE, CHM, CPFM, Editor

Custom Publishing

New York   Boston   San Francisco
London   Toronto   Sydney   Tokyo   Singapore   Madrid
Mexico City   Munich   Paris   Cape Town   Hong Kong   Montreal

**Pearson
Custom Publishing**
is a division of

PEARSON

www.pearsonhighered.com

ISBN 10: 0-558-16570-2
ISBN 13: 978-0-558-16570-3

Special Thanks

I want to thank Ed Manley for making this book possible. I also want to thank Executive Chefs Mike and Bryan for following the process outlined in this book and providing the recipes and information to complete the examples that give a "picture" of what HACCP documentation looks like.

Thanks to those who have done extensive work in creating comprehensive programs such as the one in Alaska and the program put together for schools by the National Food Service Management Institute (NFSMI) at Ole' Miss. Those programs made putting this manual together much easier and will increase the effectiveness of HACCP development and documentation.

Special thanks go out to Ron in Alaska for allowing me to include their program as a reference. Also want to thank Ron and Lorinda in Alaska for reviewing the book and providing feedback based on their experience with their own program and training.

Heartfelt thanks go out to Theresa and Virgina at NFSMI for helping me navigate the "system" for obtaining permissions to include the institute's work in the manual.

I also want to thank Alex, Bill, Bryan, Ellen, John, Kim, Mike, Robin, and other reviewers who provided feedback and helped make this a better tool.

Ann Anders

We Could Do a Better Job!

I've traveled the world teaching food safety for 6+ years, and having managed a food service association for 18 years, I've eaten in countless restaurants—fine and fast food—military, corporate, chain, Mom & Pop. And I've spent four days interacting with over 2,000 managers and workers. My perspective from all of that is, yes, we could be doing a better job, and probably would if the workers actually grasped the concept that how they act does cause, or prevent, foodborne illness.

In all the years, perhaps a handful rank as 5-Star food safety operations, another 25 as 0-Star "oh my goodness" operations, and the rest fall in the middle—doing okay and could do a little to a lot better.

Seems to me what keeps us from better protecting our customers is that people study to pass exams. Temperatures are reminded quickly and most of their time is spent memorizing bug names and terms, which won't affect their on-the-job food safety habits. I always say, "If they actually understood that their action or inaction can prevent or cause foodborne illness, they'd do better." Not washing hands and a customer getting sick, despite the exam questions, is not a leap of knowledge most have made because it gets lost in the pages of somewhat irrelevant material.

So, I met Ann and she wanted to write a high level book about HACCP, one showing her vast experience in the field. But I told her what the world needs is a simple book explaining that HACCP is actually quite logical, and quite a simple process to understand and do. The test may be complicated, but the process isn't. So we got one half of this book.

Later, I wanted a similarly simple book with sufficient information to enable people to pass a test on the subject, but not so much that we lose the simple message of what it takes to provide safe food. Ann estimated a 150-page book, and I gave her 64 to tell the story. "How many pages does it take to cover receive safe food, hold it to proper temperature, wash your hands, clean and sanitize the cutting board, etc.?" And thus KISS was born.

I believe Ann did an awesome job of providing the technical data in an easy manner. I expect you will agree and will find both parts of this book, HACCP and Food Safety, to be immensely useful to both your managers and workers, whether they are preparing for a test or preparing good and safe food. Enjoy! And thank you for letting us be a part of your food safety program.

Table of Contents

Appendices

You have read and studied how implementing a Hazard Analysis and Critical Control Point (HACCP) plan is a key element of a **Food Safety Management System** in ensuring you are delivering safe food to your consumer. You may have even taken a Certified HACCP Manager (CHM) course. After all the reading and studying, the most frequently asked questions are, "How do I get started?," "Where do I start?" or "How do I do this?"

In the wide variety of resource materials there doesn't seem to be a *single* "How to" guide. Why is that? The primary reason is that to develop an all inclusive guide of every possible food service activity would result in a gargantuan volume that would probably get more use as a door stop or car jack than as a reference guide.

Apart from your own facility, think for a moment just how many food service establishments there are and the great diversity of "types" of food that are served. Now imagine the vast number of different processes used to prepare and serve/deliver food. There are the hot dog carts or deli's on one end of the spectrum. In the middle are mid-size places that include chain restaurants and family owned establishments. The large mass producing establishments are on the other end of the spectrum. Some are only open a few hours or just for certain events, while others are open 24-hours. With such diversity, there is no one "cookie cutter" or "one-size-fits-all" template. Don't despair, we believe there is an underlying fundamental way of putting a program together and this Manual will assist you in creating your program.

This Manual will not reiterate all the details of the HACCP principles[1] and program explained in the cited references. Instead, this Manual is set up in an outline format of HACCP as discussed in the references. It will bring together charts, questions, tables and other useful program development information. This Manual is a compilation of multiple resources into one place as a single source document. The Manual will provide various checklists, sample Standard Operating Procedures (SOP), and reference tables to facilitate the flow of information for you to create your own plan. Locations for the details of specific information on some topics will be noted for direct, easy reference and additional details.

The most frequently asked questions are: "How do I get started?" "Where do I start?" or "How do I do this?"

It is important to note that HACCP is not a "magical" stand alone program. It is part of an **integration of operational practices such as sanitation, employee training, and other prerequisite programs**[3]. In reality, many of you may already have some form of the HACCP principles in place as part of your good operational practices and don't realize it.

Secondly, it is also important to remember that the "plan" is only the beginning of the process. Once the plan is documented it must be implemented. The MOST IMPORTANT thing to remember is that your HACCP plan is a "Living Document." It will change when your menu or processes change; consequently it must be continually updated. Initially the process of documenting and putting a **food safety management system** in place is labor intensive; however, don't make it any harder than it has to be.

Active Managerial Control is a term sometimes used in place of HACCP. It is described as *"the purposeful incorporation of specific actions or procedures by industry management into the operation of your business to attain control over foodborne illness risk factors"*[2].

The key is to think of the FOOD FLOW. . . the path that food follows from farmer to final sale to the consumer. This is what you do every day. . . it is the things you already know how to do. Our goal is to help you organize and create a **documented** plan that will ensure you are doing everything you possibly can to provide a safe product to the consumer.

There are literally volumes of information regarding the details of the HACCP principles and program. This Manual makes the following assumptions that management and staff:

■ Are trained and well versed in food safety; have taken a Conference for Food Protection (CFP) recognized food safety manager certification course or other food safety courses or certifications.

■ Have read and studied 7 HACCP Principles. Helpful, although not required is a Certified HACCP Manager course.

■ Have good sanitation programs in place.

■ Have an employee training program.

■ Have other prerequisite programs in place or in development (page 8).

> Our goal
> is to help you
> organize and create
> a documented plan.
> What we are doing is
> designing a process
> that will find all of the
> hazards that we might
> encounter in the food,
> and then establishing
> methods of ensuring
> that we, in fact, met
> those standards.
> Find, fix, check.

As previously mentioned there are numerous resources and reference materials regarding HACCP. The **FDA Food Code** is a good resource and should be kept on hand as a reference. It provides answers to many questions as well as has several forms that can be modeled. The primary resources used in this manual are listed below.

Because of the importance of these references, we are placing them up front in our Manual, unlike traditional footnoting or end of document reference listing. We highly recommend you print reference #2 and keep it with this Manual. In order to keep this Manual streamlined and focused on the *process* of documenting your plan, you will be given specific pages to refer to when greater details may be needed. Reference #4 is an automated SOP program; a printed copy of reference #5 can be used in conjunction with it when you are ready to create your SOPs...use the best of both to create what works for your particular establishment.

Reference	Comment	Ref. #
Hazard Analysis and Critical Control Point Principles and Application Guidelines, Aug 1997 http://www.cfsan.fda.gov/~comm/nacmcfp.html	The foundation of HACCP Principles.	1
Managing Food Safety: A Manual for the Voluntary Use of HACCP Principles for Operators of Food Service and Retail Establishments July 2005 - 85 pages http://www.cfsan.fda.gov/~dms/hret2toc.html	Manual from Food Code, "Operator's Manual" *Good resource*	2
FDA Food Code, Annex 4: Management of Food Safety Practices-Achieving Active Managerial Control of Foodborne Illness risk factors http://www.cfsan.fda.gov/~dms/	Annex from the Food Code that closely correlates with Ref #2	3
Active Managerial Control (AMC) http://www.dec.state.ak.us/eh/fss/amc/amcbroch.htm *Automated program that provides AMC training and has 16 SOP templates, 10 logs, 29 posters, and a self-assessment template. Download and use – it's that simple!*	Program established by Alaska. It is an automated system. *Excellent resource*	4
U. S. Dept. Of Agriculture, Food & Nutrition Service, & National Food Services Management Institute. (2005). HACCP-Based Standard Operating Procedures (SOPs). University, MS: Author http://sop.nfsmi.org/HACCPBasedSOPs.php *A 123 page document with 21 SOPs, 9 record keeping templates, 8 program worksheets. It has a 5-page summary of Corrective Actions, no need to "reinvent the wheel"!*	*Excellent resource!* Even though created for the schools system, the information can be used in the retail environment.	5

The FDA Food Code is a good resource and should be kept on hand.

We highly recommend you print reference #2 and keep it with this Manual.

The Basics

Here is a reminder of the five broad categories on which your Active Managerial Control efforts should focus:

Foodborne Illness Risk Factors

 **Food from unsafe sources**

 **Inadequate cooking**

 **Improper holding temperatures**

Here is a reminder of the five broad categories on which your Active Managerial Control efforts should focus.

 **Contaminated equipment**

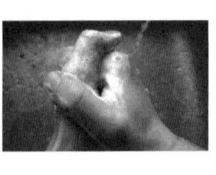 **Poor personal hygiene**

#1   Conduct a Hazard Analysis

#2   Identify the Critical Control Points (CCPs)

#3   Establish the Critical Limits (CLs)

#4   Establish Procedures to Monitor CCPs

#5   Develop Corrective Actions

#6   Establish Verification Procedures

#7   Establish a Record Keeping System

7 HACCP Principles

Details of these can be found in Ref #1, summary in Ref #2, page 9.

Introduction to the "Process Approach"

Initially, HACCP was product-specific which was extremely laborious and difficult to implement at the retail level. The evolution of the program has resulted in a "process approach[2]". Systematically you

- Divide the many food flows into broad categories based on activities or stages in the flow of food through the establishment
- Analyze the hazards
- Place managerial controls on each category

Stay with me now, the activities or stages are nothing more than operational steps, examples are:

Receive ⇨ Store ⇨ Prepare ⇨ Cook ⇨ Cool ⇨ Reheat ⇨ Hold ⇨ Assemble ⇨ Package ⇨ Serve or Sell

Nothing new . . . get the picture?

What is the Process Approach?

This may be your first exposure to the "process approach" now being recommended by the FDA. The following paragraphs explain the concept in detail. This segment is included in its entirety directly from reference #2 to ensure you grasp the concept displayed in the diagram and example that follow.

A summary of the three food preparation processes in terms of number of times through the temperature danger zone can be depicted in a Danger Zone diagram (page 4). Note that while foods produced using **Process 1** may enter the danger zone, they are *neither cooked to destroy pathogens, nor are they held hot.*

Foods that go through the danger zone only once are classified as Same Day Service, while foods that go through more than once are classified as Complex food preparation. (Don't let the "process classifications" confuse you...they simply represent the three processes based on number of times food passes through the temperature danger zone!)

The **three food preparation processes** conducted in retail and food service establishments are not intended to be all-inclusive. For instance, quick service facilities may have "cook and serve" processes specific to their operation. These processes are likely to be different from the "Same Day Service" preparation processes in full service restaurants where many of their foods are cooked and held hot before service. In addition, in retail food stores, operational steps such as packaging and assembly may be included in all of the food preparation processes prior to being delivered to the consumer.

It is also very common for a retail or food service operator to have a menu item (i.e. chicken salad sandwich) that is created by combining several components produced *using more than one kind of food preparation process.* For example, you cooked the chicken and chilled it for later use in chicken salad. And you prepared the chicken salad and then probably chilled it for later use in the making of the sandwich. It is **important for you to remember** that even though variations of the three food preparation process flows are common, the **control measures** (actions or activities that can be used to prevent, eliminate, or reduce food safety hazards) *to be implemented in each process will generally be the same based on the number of times the food goes through the temperature danger zone.*

> The control measures will generally be the same based on the number of times the food goes through the temperature danger zone.

The Process

Three preparation processes

Remember, the process categories were determined by the number of times the food passed through the temperature danger zone between 41° F to 135° F.

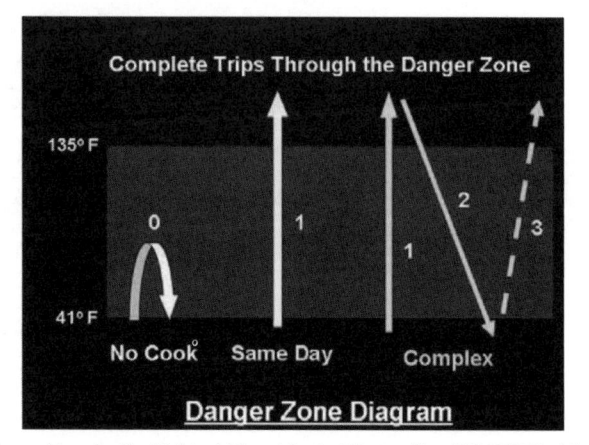

(Source: Managing Food Safety: A Manual for the Voluntary Use of HACCP Principles for Operators of Food Service and Retail Establishments)

Process 1:
No Cook Step

Food Preparation with No Cook Step

Example flow: Receive ⇨ Store ⇨ Prepare ⇨ Hold ⇨ Serve

Example: There is no cook step to destroy pathogens, such as salad, Steak Tartare or Ceviche.

Process 2:
Same Day Service

Food Preparation for Same Day Service

Example flow: Receive ⇨ Store ⇨ Prepare ⇨ Cook ⇨ Hold ⇨ Serve

Example: You cook the food, serve it, and discard what is not served.

Process 3:
Complex

Food Prepared for Later Use

Example flow: Receive ⇨ Store ⇨ Prepare ⇨ Cook ⇨ Cool ⇨ Reheat ⇨ Hot Hold ⇨ Serve

Example: There are always two or more complete trips through the temperature danger zone. You cook the food, chill it to hold for later use, re-heat and serve it. Or you have leftovers and you chill those to 41° or below for use the next day. *Note: see page 12 for sample.*

Of course there are sub-steps in the preparation of recipes — you might prepare certain items and chill them for later use in a recipe like lasagna where the sauce was probably made earlier and chilled.

The example on the following page is directly from page 16 of reference #2 and shows the process approach to conducting a hazard analysis.

An establishment has dozens of food items (including baked chicken and meatloaf) in the "Preparation for Same Day Service" category. Each of the food items may have unique hazards, but regardless of their individual hazards, control via **proper cooking** and **holding** will generally ensure the safety of all of the foods in this category. An illustration of this concept follows:

EXAMPLE:
Process approach to conducting a hazard analysis.

- Even though they have unique hazards, both baked chicken and meatloaf are either process 2 or 3 depending on your operating style.

- Salmonella and Campylobacter, as well as spore-formers, such as Bacillus cereus and Clostridium perfringens, are significant biological hazards in chicken.

- Significant biological hazards in meatloaf include Salmonella, E. coli O157:H7, Bacillus cereus, and Clostridium perfringens.

- Despite their different hazards, the **control measure** used to kill pathogens in both these products should be **cooking to the proper temperature.**

- Additionally, if the products are held after cooking, then proper hot holding or time control is also recommended to prevent the outgrowth of spore-formers that are not destroyed by cooking.

As with product-specific HACCP, **critical limits for cooking remain specific to each food item in the process.** In the scenario described above, the cooking step for chicken requires a final internal temperature of 165 °F for 15 seconds to control the pathogen load for Salmonella. Meatloaf, on the other hand, is a ground beef product and requires a final internal temperature of 155°F for 15 seconds to control the pathogen load for both Salmonella and E. coli O157:H7. Note that there are some operational steps, such as refrigerated storage or hot holding that have critical limits that apply to all foods.

PROCESS 2: Preparation for Same Day Service

Example Products	Meatloaf	Chicken
Example Biological Hazards	Salmonella E. coli O157:H7 Clostridium perfringens Bacillus cereus Various fecal-oral route pathogens	Salmonella Campylobacter Clostridium perfringens Bacillus cereus Various fecal-oral route pathogens
Example Control Measures *there may be others*	• **Cooking at 155°F for 15 seconds** • Refrigeration 41°F or below • Hot Holding at 135°F or above OR Time Control for 4 hours or less • No bare hand contact with RTE food, proper hand-washing, exclusion/restriction of ill employees	• **Cooking at 165°F for 15 seconds** • Refrigeration 41°F or below • Hot Holding at 135°F or above OR Time Control for 4 hours or less • No bare hand contact with RTE food, proper hand washing, exclusion/restriction of ill employees

Pages 18 - 20
in Reference #2
provide
good examples

(Source: Managing Food Safety: A Manual for the Voluntary Use of HACCP Principles for Operators of Food Service and Retail Establishments)

Developing Your Food Safety Management System

Here is the recommended progression of events:

Begin with Prerequisite Programs in place

▼

- *Assemble* a HACCP Team ➤
- *Describe* the Product (Recipe) ➤
- *Identify* the Intended Use ➤
- *Construct* the Food Flow Diagram for each recipe, from receiving to the customer ➤
- *Confirm* that the Food Flow Diagram is done correctly ➤
- *Group* recipes by Process 1, 2 or 3 ➤
- *Conduct* Hazard Analysis ➤
- *Establish* Critical Limits (CLs) for CCPs ➤
- *Establish* Control Measures for CLs ➤
- *Establish* Monitoring Procedures ➤
- *Develop* Corrective Actions (see page 99 of Ref #5) ➤
- *Conduct* Ongoing Verification of the HACCP Plan ➤
- *Keep* Extensive Records ➤
- *Conduct* Periodic Validation of the HACCP Plan

Developing Your Food Safety Management System (FSMS)

Prerequisite Programs

Prerequisite to starting a HACCP Plan is having a good food safety program in the traditional sense – the place is clean; employees are knowledgeable of food service procedures; pests are controlled; etc. Examples of Prerequisite Programs are:

Vendor certification programs

Training programs

Allergen management

Buyer specifications

Recipe/process instructions

First-In-First-Out (FIFO) procedures

Pest control program

Waste management

Other SOPs to include but not limited to:

Food source

Receiving/storage

Handwashing

Personal hygiene

Employee health

Employee training

Cleaning/sanitizing

No bare hand contact with Ready to eat (RTE) foods

Cooking

Cooling

Reheating

Cold holding

Hot holding

A sample from each of the SOP references #4 & #5 are included in Appendix 1.

Prerequisite program coverage

See Ref #2, pages 24-26 for more details

What should these programs cover? There are three broad categories you should think about when creating or reviewing your prerequisite programs:

• Control contamination of food

• Control bacterial growth

• Maintain equipment

Preliminary Steps

Preliminary Step 1

Assemble HACCP Team

The members of this team will vary from one location to another whether you are a hospital, school, small food service facility, a chain restaurant or a mega-large facility. Personnel titles in each of these facilities vary. As an example some locations have "Manager on Duty" (MOD) designations; others call them "Shift Supervisor."

The team should have representation from all areas of the operation. This may include, but not limited to, managers, supervisors, shift supervisors, shift managers, line managers, front-of-the-house managers, "lead" personnel, chefs, cooks, receiving clerks, servers, stewarding personnel, dishwashers, equipment maintenance personnel and any other members of your organization that are actively involved in preparing and serving food. Collectively, they need to know how the food is handled by the staff, which equipment is used to sauté, broil, etc.

You may also want to consider the participation of your local regulator or inspecting agency for collaboration with your HACCP team. You may want them to participate ad hoc as needed or use them as consultants.

In the various examples provided, you may see specific personnel "titles" listed; you would just insert the appropriate team member or designated individual title for your facility or type of operation.

Before going any further, let's make sure you understand the concept and can visualize it as we work through the rest of the process. The first thing the team will do is Describe the Product – which means take your standardized recipes and incorporate the flow from receiving to service to the customer, including food safety concerns. We'll use Lasagna as an example.

Describe the Product—We start with a list of ingredients (below) and the Procedure to put them together. This procedure describes *Process 3: Complex* because the product goes through the temperature danger zone three times—cold to cooked, cooked to chilled for holding, and chilled to reheat for service. Then we add the steps after preparation until the product is served or discarded.

Don't let the term "Complex Food Preparation" throw you off. A hamburger patty is complex if you cook it, chill it, and reheat it the next day. Complex means the trips through the food danger zone, not the difficulty of preparation. You might use some of the Lasagna immediately (Process 2) and refrigerate some for the night meal (Process 3).

Intended Use—Next we identify any special concerns based on your type of operation, which we call your "Intended Use." Are your customers immune deficient, kids, pregnant mothers? Are you serving buffet style or served meals? This information will help you in the Hazard Analysis step for example if the hazard is listeria and you work at a maternity hospital.

Be mindful this is a food safety book, not a cookbook, the Lasagna recipe you use may differ slightly or significantly. For continuity, we will follow this recipe through the whole process in the samples to follow. The samples are not inclusive of all details for each step but rather a representation of items to give you some reference points.

	SAMPLE RECIPE			
Ingredients	Amt.	Servings		
		25	50	100
Lasagna noodles	Lbs.	10	20	40
Ground beef meat sauce	Gals.	2	4	8
Ricotta Cheese Mix	Lbs.	8	16	32
Shredded Mozzarella	Lbs.	5	10	20
Pomodoro Sauce	Gals.	1	2	4
Fresh eggs	Ea.	6	12	24
Chopped Parsley				

Using Lasagna Example

Pre-Preparation

SOP-1   1. Wash hands before beginning food production.

SOP-1   2. Thaw ground beef under refrigeration at 41°F or below.

SOP-1   3. Clean and rinse parsley with cool running water and chop as directed. Use immediately in the recipe or cover and refrigerate at 41°F or below.

Preparation

4. Cook lasagna noodles

CCP-1   5. Cook the ground beef to an internal temperature of 155°F for a minimum of 15 seconds in a large sauce pan for approximately 30 minutes. Add pomodoro sauce and cook to an internal temperature of 155°F for a minimum of 15 seconds.

Cool

6. Cool the lasagna noodles from 135°F to 70°F within 2 hours and from 70°F to 41°F within 4 more hours.

CCP-2   7. Cool sauce in shallow pans with a product depth not to exceed 2 inches. Cool the product from 70°F within 2 hours and from 70°F to 41°F within 4 more hours.

Preparation

8. Remove ricotta cheese and fresh eggs from refrigeration and combine all ingredients and blend in a properly sanitized mixer.

9. Build lasagna in baking pans by alternating layers of lasagna noodles, cheese and meat sauce.

CCP-3   10. Bake the lasagna uncovered to an internal temperature of 155°F for a minimum of 15 seconds in a preheated convection oven at 350°F for approximately one hour.

Holding/Service

CCP-4   11. Maintain temperature of product at 135°F or higher during service period. Record temperatures of unused product every 30 minutes.

Storage

CCP-5   12. Cool in shallow pans with a product depth not to exceed 2 inches. Quick-chill the product from 135°F to 70°F within 2 hours and from 70° to 41°F within 4 more hours.

CCP-6   13. Store the lasagna in a labeled, covered container at a product temperature of 41°F or below.

Reheating

CCP-7   14. Remove from refrigeration and heat in a preheated conventional oven at 350°F. Heat until all parts of the product reach an internal temperature of 165°F for 15 seconds.

15. Discard unused product.

So, what is a Food Flow Diagram? Here and on page 25 I relate things to traffic, something with which we are more familiar. Think of the Flow Diagram as a GPS system, which identifies each of the places along the highway where you will change the direction of your car. Each time the GPS beeps and makes an announcement; that is a Control Point. Between Control Points, no action is required. You started on Elm Street, took a right at Main Street then a left at Jones Street, and you then got to your destination at Front Street. Now replace those with places in the kitchen and you have the lettuce starting at the Loading Dock, taking a right into the Refrigerator, then a left down to Veg Prep, and ultimately making it to the Serving Line. If your GPS fails to beep, what happens? You get lost. In the kitchen, what happens is that you also don't get the message about a possible hazard, therefore you don't set up standards to find and fix the hazard.

We will use that information at Principle 1, the Hazard Analysis,to determine which hazards could be present at each of those locations (Control Points).

Page 12 shows what you would call the Procedure part of a recipe card, and describes a Complex process because the product goes through the temperature danger zone three times – cold to cooked, cooked to chilled for holding, and chilled to reheat for service. We start with list of ingredients and the Procedure to put them together. Then we add the steps after preparation until the product is served or discarded.

Food Flow Diagrams—Page 14 follows the product (ground beef) from Receiving to Service. Each rectangle represents a Control Point – some of which we will later identify as Critical Control Points (CCPs). After Reheating the product would go back up to Holding/Service and would be discarded if not used.

Forms for Your Use—Followng the Food Flow Diagram, you will find some forms that the team *might* choose to use.

Preliminary Steps 4 & 5
Construct and Confirm the Food Flow Diagram

FIGURE 1. HACCP Flow Chart / Diagram

USING LASAGNA EXAMPLE

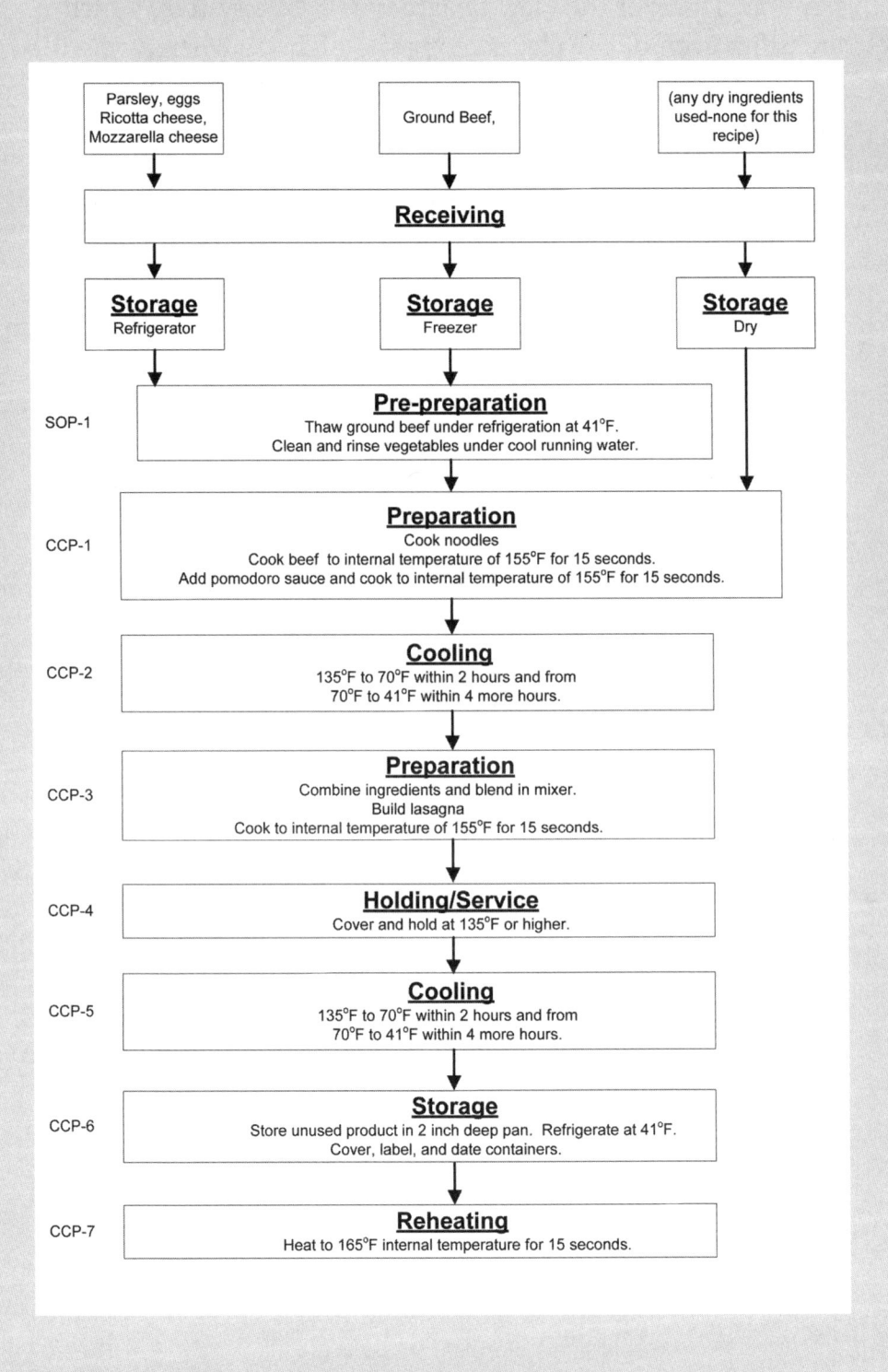

On the following pages are snapshots of the forms which are provided in Appendix 2. If you choose to use the forms, you can fill them in as you proceed through each step in the process.

You are asking, *"Do I have to use these forms?"* and the answer is "No." If you have a format that works for you by all means use it. If you are starting from scratch, these may help.

We understand that it is difficult to create a masterpiece from a blank canvas. We are going to guide you through the creation of your masterpiece by providing samples along with giving you ideas of what information is used in each area of the form.

You will note that the rows and columns of the forms match the steps in the process. **Form A** is the same for all three processes. Only **Form B** changes for each of the three processes primarily because more steps are required. You should see a correlation between the forms and the Food Flow provided on the previous pages.

You will note that the rows and columns of the forms match the steps in the process.

Form A is the same for all three processes

FORM A – Blank

MENU ITEMS/PRODUCTS:						
HAZARD(S)	**CRITICAL CONTROL POINTS (List Only the Operational Steps that are CCPs)**	**CRITICAL LIMITS**	**MONITORING**	**CORRECTIVE ACTIONS**	**VERIFICATION**	**RECORDS**
PREREQUISITE PROGRAMS						

FORM A – Completed

Form 3A
Process #3 – Complex Food Preparation

MENU ITEMS/PRODUCTS: Lasagna, Taco meat, tamales, etc.						
HAZARD(S)	**CRITICAL CONTROL POINTS (List Only the Operational Steps that are CCPs)**	**CRITICAL LIMITS**	**MONITORING**	**CORRECTIVE ACTIONS**	**VERIFICATION**	**RECORDS**
Salmonella E. Coli O 157:H7 C. perfringens Bacillus cereus	CCP – 1 & 3 COOK	155 °F for 15 seconds	Cooking Temp. log @ 30 min. & 1 hr.	Continue cooking until required internal temp. is reached.	Designated HACCP Team member will: Review receiving logs monthly. Temp. logs weekly Thermometer calibration log weekly Etc…	Vendor Guarantees SOPs Food Safety Checklist Manager Checklist Thermometer calibration log Temperature logs Quarterly, semi-annual & yearly audit sheets Etc…
	CCP – 2 & 5 COOLING	135ºF to 70ºF within 2 hrs. & 70ºF to 41ºF within 4 hrs.	Cooling Temp. log @ 2/4/6 hr. intervals	Discard cooked, hot food immediately when the food is: > 70 °F and > 2 hours into the cooling process		
	CCP – 4 HOT HOLDING	135ºF or higher	Hot Holding Temp. log @ l hr. intervals	Reheat to 165 °F for 15 sec. if temp. is <135 °F and was >135 °F or higher within the last 2 hours.		
	CCP – 6 COLD HOLDING	41ºF or below	Cold Holding Temp. log @ l hr. intervals	Discard food if can't determine how long the food temp. was >41 °F.		
	CCP – 7 REHEATING	165ºF for 15 seconds	Reheating log	Continue cooking until required internal temp. is reached.		
PREREQUISITE PROGRAMS	SOPs: Handwashing, Thawing, No Bare Hand contact with RTE, FIFO, etc… Approved source; etc…					

MENU ITEMS/PRODUCTS:
Lasagna, Taco meat, tamales, etc.

PROCESS STEP	HAZARD(S)	CCPs (Y/N)	CRITICAL LIMITS	MONITORING	CORRECTIVE ACTIONS	VERIFICATION	RECORDS
RECEIVE	*Salmonella* *E. Coli O 157:H7* *C. perfringens* *Bacillus cereus*	N #	Approved source Cold - <41°F Shellfish tags	Vendor agreement Receiving logs	Refuse product	(who) review logs weekly, verify suppliers monthly	*Vendor Guarantees *SOPs *Food Safety Checklist *Manager Checklist *Thermometer calibration log *Temperature logs *Quarterly, semi-annual & yearly audit sheets Etc...
STORE		Y	Cold - <41°F RTE above raw FIFO	Refrigerator logs Observation	Report high refrigerator temps to Engineering	(who) review logs weekly, verifies stock rotation	
PREPARE		Y ##	Thaw in cooler/under running water, no bare hand contact with RTE	Observation	Retrain employees	(who) review incident logs or training records	
COOK		Y	155 °F for 15 seconds	Cooking Temp. log @ 30 min. & 1 hr.	Continue cooking until required internal temp. is reached.	(who) review logs weekly	
COOL		Y	135°F to 70°F within 2 hrs. & 70°F to 41°F within 4 hrs.	Cooling Temp. log @ 2/4/6 hr. intervals	Discard cooked, hot food immediately when the food is: > 70 °F and > 2 hours into the cooling process	(who) review logs weekly	
REHEAT		Y	165°F for 15 seconds	Reheating log	Continue cooking until required internal temp. is reached.	(who) review logs weekly	
HOLD		Y	Hot 135°F or higher Cold 41°F or below	Temperature logs	Hot - Reheat to 165 °F for 15 sec. if temp. is <135 °F and was >135 °F or higher within the last 2 hours. Cold - Discard food if can't determine how long the food temp. was >41 °F.	(who) review logs weekly	
SERVE		Y ##	Proper handwashing No bare hand contact Cleaning/sanitizing Exclusion of ill staff	Observation	Retrain employees	Observation (who) review incident logs or training records	
PREREQUISITE PROGRAMS	SOPs: Handwashing, Thawing, No Bare Hand contact with RTE, FIFO, etc... Approved source; etc... # This could be an example of where your receiving SOP is used and that receiving is not a CCP. This will depend on the way you run your operation. ## Things like handwashing, cleaning and sanitizing SOPs would also apply.						

Process #1

PROCESS STEP
RECEIVE
STORE
PREPARE
HOLD
SERVE

Process #2

PROCESS STEP
RECEIVE
STORE
PREPARE
COOK
HOLD
SERVE

Process #3

PROCESS STEP
RECEIVE
STORE
PREPARE
COOK
COOL
REHEAT
HOLD
SERVE

For **Form B** you will notice that the **Process Step** column is different for each of the three processes while the remaining columns are essentially the same as **Form A**.

Group Menu Items/ Products

Utilizing the Food Flow Diagrams (p. 14) you will now group your menu items into Process 1, 2, or 3 depending on how the products will be used. A reminder of three Process categories:

PROCESS 1: Food Preparation with No Cook Step

Example flow:
Receive ⇨ Store ⇨ Prepare ⇨ Hold ⇨ Serve

PROCESS 2: Preparation for Same Day Service

Example flow:
Receive ⇨ Store ⇨ Prepare ⇨ Cook ⇨ Hold ⇨ Serve

PROCESS 3: Complex Food Preparation

Example flow:
Receive ⇨ Store ⇨ Prepare ⇨ Cook ⇨ Cool ⇨ Reheat ⇨ Hot Hold – Serve

PROCESS #1 Cook Step Food Preparation with No Cook Step	PROCESS #2 Service Food Preparation for Same Day	PROCESS #3 Preparation Complex Food
• raw meat and seafood (to be cooked by consumer) • salad greens • fish for raw consumption • fresh vegetables • oysters or clams served raw • tuna salad • Caesar salad dressing • Cole slaw • sliced sandwich meats • sliced cheese • salad (made from canned chicken)	• fried chicken • broiled fish • fried oysters • hamburgers • soup du jour • hot vegetables • cooked eggs	• soups • gravies • sauces • large roasts • chili • taco filling • egg rolls • chicken salad (made from raw chicken)

(Source: Managing Food Safety: A Manual for the Voluntary Use of HACCP Principles for Operators of Food Service and Retail Establishments)

Complete a sheet for each of the 3 processes listing the items.

MENU ITEMS/PRODUCTS: Lasagna, Taco meat, tamales, etc. ⇦ Complete						
HAZARD(S)	CRITICAL CONTROL POINTS (List Only the Operational Steps that are CCPs)	CRITICAL LIMITS	MONITORING	CORRECTIVE ACTIONS	VERIFICATION	RECORDS

HACCP Implementation – a Quick Reference Manual

HACCP Principles

Principle 1
Conduct Hazard Analysis

HACCP Principle #1

"The purpose of hazard analysis is to develop a list of food safety hazards that are reasonably likely to cause illness or injury if not effectively controlled."[3]

This is where your HACCP team must work closely together and have a "brainstorming" session. Simply put, the team figures out what possible hazards there are, all the way from the farm to the consumer, and determines what control measures must be implemented to make sure you prevent, eliminate or reduce the hazards to an acceptable level. Control measures are nothing more than "What steps or actions do you take to prevent, eliminate or reduce the hazards?"

Put another way, there are two stages: **identify** the hazard and then **evaluate** it. When evaluating the hazard you are looking for the severity of the potential hazard and how likely is it to occur. Table 1 on page 23 provides *"Examples of How the Stages of Hazard Analysis are used to Identify and Evaluate Hazards."*[1] It may give you some ideas on how to proceed.

You may be saying I don't know where to begin to identify or evaluate the possible hazards for my establishment. We have assembled tables (from the different references) that encompass the majority of the biological, chemical and physical hazards that have been identified. The seven tables are in Appendix 3 to 9 of this Manual. The team may identify some that are very specific to your establishment once they get started.

If the team needs a refresher on conducting the analysis, Reference #2 (pages 28-30 and Annex 3 on page 70) and Reference #3 (pages 480-488) provide detailed discussion on this topic.

What do you need in the brainstorming session? We recommend that you have three process forms provided in Appendix 2, copies of the tables in Appendix 3 – 9, and the list of questions on page 22 & Appendix 10, to help with conducting the hazard analysis.

Complete the Hazard(s) column.

HAZARD(S)	CRITICAL CONTROL POINTS (List Only the Operational Steps that are CCPs)	CRITICAL LIMITS	MONITORING	CORRECTIVE ACTIONS	VERIFICATION	RI
Salmonella E. Coli O157:H7 C. perfringens Bacillus cereus	CCP – 1 & 3 COOK	155 °F for 15 seconds	Cooking Temp. log @ 30 min. & 1 hr.	Continue cooking until required internal temp. is reached.	Designated HACCP Team member will: Review receiving	Vendor SOPs Food S Manag

From the retail perspective, you are considered the "last line of defense" for serving safe food. It is up to you to prevent the hazards. As a reminder, the hazards and some examples are:

1) Biological
- Bacteria & their toxins
- Parasites
- Viruses

2) Physical
- Stones/pebbles/dirt
- Glass
- Bone and metal fragments
- Packaging materials

3) Chemical
- Natural plant and animal toxins
- Unlabeled allergens
- Cleaning compounds
- Insecticides

Stage 1: Identify Hazards

"Hazards are defined as a biological, chemical, or physical property that may cause a food to be unsafe for human consumption." [3]

Specific Biological Food Safety Hazards

Below are some of the biological hazards found in common products. We DO need to know the names of the various bacteria, and what those bacteria are likely to do to us (vomitting, diarrhea), so that when someone gets sick, we can evaluate the cause and the action to take to fix the problem and prevent it in the future.

- *Salmonella* and *Campylobacter jejuni* in raw poultry
- *Salmonella Enteriditis* in undercooked eggs
- *E. coli O157:H7* in raw ground beef
- *Listeria monocytogenes* in ready-to-eat foods, such as hot dogs and deli meat
- Bacterial pathogens associated with unpasteurized juice or milk
- *Staphylococcus aureus* toxin formation in ready-to-eat products that are contaminated and later temperature-abused, such as cooked ham
- *Bacillus cereus* spore survival and toxin formation in cooked rice
- *Clostridium perfringens* and *B. cereus* spore survival and subsequent growth in cooked meat/meat products

Stage 2:
Evaluate Hazards

Questions to ask to evaluate food safety hazards:

- Is the food from a safe source?

- Do food workers practice good personal hygiene, including frequent and effective handwashing?

- Has the food been exposed to unclean or unsanitized equipment?

- Is the Supply Chain likely to add hazards (such as E. coli in produce)?

- Are there any ingredients or menu items of special concern such as those listed in the tables?

- Is this a potentially hazardous food requiring specific temperature controls?

- How will it be served? Immediately? Held on a buffet?

- Does this food have a history of being associated with illnesses?

- Will this require a great deal of preparation, making preparation time, employee health, and bare hand contact with ready-to-eat food a special concern?

- How will employees exhibiting symptoms such as diarrhea or vomiting be handled?

- Are you serving food to a population that is known to be highly susceptible to foodborne illness (e.g., residents of health care facilities, persons in child or adult day care facilities, etc.)?

- Does the food permit survival or multiplication of pathogens and/or toxin formation in the food before or during preparation?

- Will the food permit survival or multiplication of pathogens and/or toxin formation during subsequent steps of preparation?

- What has been the safety record for the product in the marketplace? Is there an epidemiological history associated with this food?

- What is known about the time/temperature exposure of the food?

- What is the water activity and pH of the food?

- Have bare hands touched the food, or otherwise cross-contaminated it?

- Does the preparation procedure or process include a step that destroys pathogens or their toxins? (Consider both vegetative cells and spores)

- Is the product subject to recontamination after cooking?

There are additional questions in Appendix 10.

(Source: Managing Food Safety:
A Manual for the Voluntary Use of HACCP Principles for Operators of Food Service and Retail Establishments)

TABLE 1 – Examples of How the Stages of Hazard Analysis are used to Identify and Evaluate Hazards*

Hazard Analysis Stage		Frozen cooked beef patties produced in a manufacturing plant	Product containing eggs prepared for foodservice	Commercial frozen pre-cooked, boned chicken for further processing
Stage 1 Hazard Identification	*Determine potential hazards associated with product*	Enteric pathogens (i.e., E. coli O157:H7 and Salmonella)	Salmonella in finished product.	Staphylococcus aureus in finished product.
Stage 2 Hazard Evaluation	*Assess severity of health consequences if potential hazard is not properly controlled.*	Epidemiological evidence indicates that these pathogens cause severe health effects including death among children and elderly. Undercooked beef patties have been linked to disease from these pathogens.	Salmonellosis is a food borne infection causing a moderate to severe illness that can be caused by ingestion of only a few cells of Salmonella.	Certain strains of S. aureus produce an enterotoxin which can cause a moderate foodborne illness.
	Determine likelihood of occurrence of potential hazard if not properly controlled.	E. coli O157:H7 is of very low probability and salmonellae is of moderate probability in raw meat.	Product is made with liquid eggs which have been associated with past outbreaks of Salmonellosis. Recent problems with Salmonella serotype Enteriditis in eggs cause increased concern. Probability of Salmonella in raw eggs cannot be ruled out. If not effectively controlled, some consumers are likely to be exposed to Salmonella from this food.	Product may be contaminated with S. aureus due to human handling during boning of cooked chicken. Enterotoxin capable of causing illness will only occur as S. aureus multiplies to about 1,000,000/g. Operating procedures during boning and subsequent freezing prevent growth of S. aureus, thus the potential for enterotoxin formation is very low.
	Using information above, determine if this potential hazard is to be addressed in the HACCP plan.	The HACCP team decides that enteric pathogens are hazards for this product. **Hazards must be addressed in the plan.**	HACCP team determines that if the potential hazard is not properly controlled, consumption of product is likely to result in an unacceptable health risk. **Hazard must be addressed in the plan.**	The HACCP team determines that the potential for enterotoxin formation is very low. However, it is still desirable to keep the initial number of S. aureus organisms low. Employee practices that minimize contamination, rapid carbon dioxide freezing and handling instructions have been adequate to control this potential hazard. **Potential hazard does not need to be addressed in plan.**

* For illustrative purposes only. The potential hazards identified may not be the only hazards associated with the products listed. The responses may be different for different establishments.

(Source: Appendix D of Reference #1 - Hazard Analysis and Critical Control Point Principles and Application Guidelines)

Hazard Analysis – Risk and Severity

Risk is the likelihood that an adverse health effect will occur within a population as a result of a hazard in a food.

So what does that mean? You have to look at your customer population, the type of food you serve, along with the size of your operation and turnover of staff.

For example, if a facility is small and has a limited menu, the risk is less than that of a larger facility with more menu items and more food handling.

Keeping the staff trained is a big challenge to ensure everyone knows of the hazards and how to prevent them.

Severity is the degree of seriousness of the consequences of exposure to the hazard.

To determine the severity one has to be aware of the medical impact of a hazard on a person.

For instance, Norovirus will make an average person miserable for 2 or 3 days. Whereas, botulism can kill!

Now let's take the same hazard in two different populations – E. coli in a normal, healthy person will give them significant gastric distress for a couple of days. In a young, old or compromised person, it could be deadly because of possible kidney failure.

Keep in mind that if hazards are not likely to occur, they do not need to be addressed by an HACCP program.

> Keep in mind that if hazards are not likely to occur, they do not need to be addressed by an HACCP program.

Think of the Control Points as intersections and the Decision Tree as a tool to help you decide which ones need a stop sign to ensure safety. If an intersection (control point) is where you will have an accident if you don't stop the car and observe the situation, then you designate that as a Critical Control Point, and place a stop sign there. The Decision Tree helped you to decide where to put stop signs (Critical Control Points). So then, what indication do you have that you put the stop signs at the right locations? You didn't have any accidents along that route. If you DID have an accident, then you would review the process and perhaps add another stop sign (CCP).

A reminder of what the *operational steps* are:

Receive ⇨ Store ⇨ Prepare ⇨ Cook ⇨ Cool ⇨ Reheat ⇨ Hold ⇨ Assemble ⇨ Package ⇨ Serve or Sell

Now that the Hazard Analysis shows us what the hazards are, we need to look at the Control Points on the Flow Diagram and select those that are Critical.

Decision Tree —the Decision Tree is used to decide which Control Points are Critical. Figure 2 on page 36 is the Decision Tree as adapted from NACMCF from Reference #3. Follow the decision tree answering the questions in sequence for each step in the process.

CCPs should focus on foodborne disease risk factors:

1. Time/Temperature

   • Cooking   • Cooling

   • Holding   • Reheating

2. Employee Health/Habits

3. Cross Contamination

Principle 2
Determine Critical Control Points

HACCP Principle #2

Determine Critical Control Points (CCPs)

"By definition, a CCP is an operational step at which control can be applied and is essential to prevent or eliminate a hazard or reduce it to an acceptable level,"[2] thereby ensuring that we have effectively controlled the hazard.

Complete the CCP column.

HAZARD(S)	CRITICAL CONTROL POINTS (List Only the Operational Steps that are CCPs)	CRITICAL LIMITS	MONITORING	CORRECTIVE ACTIONS	VERIFICATION	RE
Salmonella E. Coli O157:H7 C. perfringens Bacillus cereus	CCP – 1 & 3 COOK	155 °F for 15 seconds	Cooking Temp. log @ 30 min. & 1 hr.	Continue cooking until required internal temp. is reached.	Designated HACCP Team member will: Review receiving logs monthly.	Vendor SOPs Food Sa Manager Thermor cal
	CCP – 2 & 5 COOLING	135°F to 70°F within 2 hrs. & 70°F to 41°F within 4 hrs.	Cooling Temp. log @ 2/4/6 hr. intervals	Discard cooked, hot food immediately when the food is: > 70 °F and > 2 hours into the cooling process	Temp. logs weekly Thermometer calibration log weekly Etc...	Temper e Quarterl ann aud Etc...

FIGURE 2. CCP Decision Tree 1 (Adapted from NACMCF)[3]

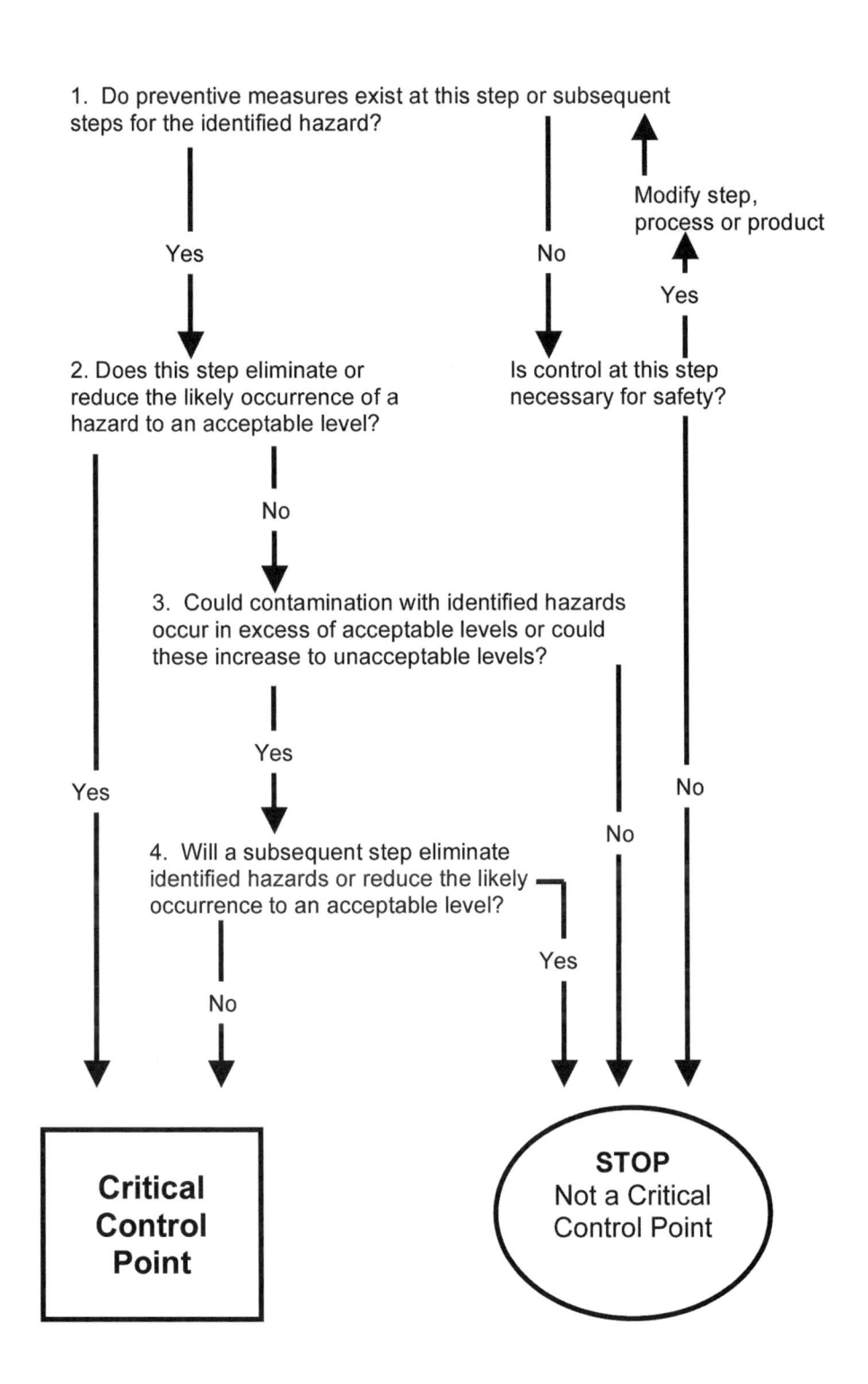

Follow the decision tree answering the questions in sequence for each step in the process.

Critical Limits define the point at which food is acceptable. If the Critical Limit is 165° or higher and the food is 165° the product is acceptable.

Critical Limits (CLs) must have Control Measures - those actions taken which get the product to the Critical Limit, such as cooking is the control measure for a CL of 165°. Washing is the Control Measure for a CL of no dirt in the lettuce. Otherwise, you must change the process by which you deal with that issue, such as maybe washing the lettuce twice.

Below are some samples of CCPs with Critical Limits. Chart 1 and Chart 2 provide the temperature limits as stated in the Food Code.

PRODUCT: Ground meat or eggs not prepared for immediate use
CCP: Cooking
CL: 155°F for 15 seconds

PRODUCT: Refried beans
CCP: Reheating
CL: 165°F within 2 hours

PRODUCT: Beef chili
CCP: Cooling
CL: 135°F to 70°F within 2 hours, 70°F to 41°F in 4 more hours, total of . . .
or less 135°F to 41°F.

PRODUCT: Whole roast beef
CCP: Holding
CL: 130°F or above / or 41°F or below

PRODUCT: Sushi rice
CCP: Holding
CL: 135°F or pH 4.6

PRODUCT: Oysters (Served raw)
CCP: Receiving
CL: Product must be from an approved source

Complete the CL for each CCP, insert into form.

HAZARD(S)	CRITICAL CONTROL POINTS (List Only the Operational Steps that are CCPs)	CRITICAL LIMITS	MONITORING	CORRECTIVE ACTIONS	VERIFICATION	F
Salmonella E. Coli O157:H7 C. perfringens Bacillus cereus	CCP – 1 & 3 COOK	155 °F for 15 seconds	Cooking Temp. log @ 30 min. & 1 hr.	Continue cooking until required internal temp. is reached.	Designated HACCP Team member will: Review receiving logs monthly. Temp. logs weekly Thermometer calibration log weekly Etc...	Vendc SOPs Food Mana; Therm c Tempe Quart(a Etc...
	CCP – 2 & 5 COOLING	135°F to 70°F within 2 hrs. & 70°F to 41°F within 4 hrs.	Cooling Temp. log @ 2/4/6 hr. intervals	Discard cooked, hot food immediately when the food is: > 70 °F and > 2 hours into the cooling process		

Principle 3
Establish Critical Limits

HACCP Principle #3
What is a *Critical Limit* and what is it's purpose?

"… a prescribed parameter (e.g., minimum and/or maximum value) that must be met to ensure that food safety hazards are controlled at each CCP … used to separate acceptable from unacceptable food.

"Each control measure at a CCP has one or more associated critical limits.

"Critical limits may be based upon factors like temperature, time, moisture level, water activity (a_w), or pH" [(quantitative) or things like chicken skin not sticky, fish not smelling, eyes clear (qualitative)].

"They must be scientifically-based and measurable."[3]

CHART 1. Summary Chart for Minimum Cooking Food Temperatures and Holding Times

Required by Chapter 3 of Food Code

(Source: Appendix 7 *Model Forms, Guides, and Other Aids*)

Food	Minimum Temperature	Minimum Holding Time at the Specified Temperature
Raw Eggs prepared for immediate service **Commercially Raised Game Animals and Exotic Species of Game Animals Fish, Pork, and Meat** Not Otherwise Specified in this Chart or in & 3-401.11(B)	145°F	15 seconds
Raw Eggs not prepared for immediate service **Comminuted (ground) Commercially Raised Game Animals and** **Exotic Species of Game Animals** **Comminuted (ground) Fish and Meats** **Injected Meats**	155°F 155°F 150°F 145°F	< 1 second 15 seconds 1 minute 3 minutes
Poultry **Baluts** **Stuffed Fish; Stuffed Meat;** **Stuffed Pasta;** **Stuffed Poultry; Stuffed Ratites** **Stuffing Containing Fish, Meat,** **Poultry, or Ratites** **Wild Game Animals**	165°F	15 seconds
Food Cooked in A **Microwave Oven**	165°F	and hold for 2 minutes after removing from microwave oven

CHART 2. Summary Chart for Minimum Food Temperatures and Holding Times

Required by Chapter 3 of the Food Code for Reheating Foods for Hot Holding

(Source: Appendix 7 *Model Forms, Guides, and Other Aids*)

Food	Minimum Temperature	Minimum Holding Time at the Specified Temperature	Maximum Time to Reach Minimum Temperature
¶ 3-403.11(A) and (D) Food that is cooked, cooled, and reheated	165°F	15 seconds	2 hours
¶ 3-403.11(B) and (D) Food that is reheated in a microwave oven	165°F	and hold for 2 minutes after reheating	2 hours
¶ 3-403.11(C) and (D) Food that is taken from a commercially processed, hermetically sealed container or intact package	135°F	No time specified	2 hours
¶ 3-403.11(E) Unsliced portions of meat roasts cooked as specified under ¶ 3-401.11(B)	Same oven parameters and minimum time and temperature conditions as specified under ¶ 3-401.11(B)		Not applicable
	OR		
	Minimum and maximum time and temperature conditions listed in this chart for ¶3-403.11(A), and (D).		

The purpose of monitoring is to determine whether the critical limits that have been established for each CCP are being met.

How you monitor depends on the Critical Limit. You wouldn't check for dirt in the lettuce by taking the temperature of the lettuce; you would observe the lettuce. Examples include visual observations and measurements of time, temperature, pH, and water activity.

Consideration should be given to determining answers to the following questions:

- What will you monitor?
- How will you monitor?
- When and how often will you monitor?
- Who will be responsible for monitoring?
- Where and how will we record the results of the monitoring?
- Who will follow-up on the logs to be sure they have been completed honestly, with counter-signatures, reviewed by management, etc.?
- Will our monitoring records be pieces of paper to be filed and never seen again, or actively used histories of the past, which will be used to predict the future and ensure safe food?

While some things, like monitoring a Critical Limit of 145° for soup, are easy, others require training — like a Critical Limit of 165° for a whole turkey requires training to avoid hitting the bone with your thermometer, which would give a false reading, or checking fish for smell or clear eyes.

Just as the *use* of knowledge is power, so too the immediate action taken when monitoring shows problems is key. Monitoring without resulting action is a paperwork exercise.

HACCP Principle #4

"Monitoring is the act of observing and making measurements to help determine if critical limits are being met and maintained."[3]

"Monitoring will identify when there is a loss of control or a trend toward a loss of control so that corrective actions can be taken."[2]

Complete the Monitoring column.

HAZARD(S)	CRITICAL CONTROL POINTS (List Only the Operational Steps that are CCPs)	CRITICAL LIMITS	MONITORING	CORRECTIVE ACTIONS	VERIFICATION	R
Salmonella E. Coli O157:H7 C. perfringens Bacillus cereus	CCP – 1 & 3 COOK	155 °F for 15 seconds	Cooking Temp. log @ 30 min. & 1 hr.	Continue cooking until required internal temp. is reached.	Designated HACCP Team member will: Review receiving logs monthly. Temp. logs weekly Thermometer calibration log weekly Etc...	Vendor SOPs Food S Manag Thermo c Temper Quarte an Etc...
	CCP – 2 & 5 COOLING	135°F to 70°F within 2 hrs. & 70°F to 41°F within 4 hrs.	Cooling Temp. log @ 2/4/6 hr. intervals	Discard cooked, hot food immediately when the food is: > 70 °F and > 2 hours into the cooling process		

Principle 5
Develop Corrective Actions

HACCP Principle #5

"Corrective actions are activities that are taken by a person whenever a critical limit is not met"[3] at a Critical Control Point.

Simple samples of corrective actions are discarding food that could pose a threat or rejecting a shipment of raw oysters without tags, and determining how to safely discard those oysters so they don't create a hazard for "dumpster divers" or be found and used by staff.

Reference #3 recommends that you can decide what type of corrective action to take if a critical limit is not met by asking yourself the following questions:

- What measures do you expect employees to take to correct the problem?

- Do your employees understand the corrective action?

- Can the corrective action be easily implemented?

- Are different options needed for the appropriate corrective actions depending on the process and monitoring frequency?

- How will these corrective actions be documented and communicated to management so the system can be modified to prevent the problem from occurring again?

- Of course, things invariably go wrong when the key staff is off Sunday morning. Leave nothing to chance, be sure the HACCP Plan covers emergencies and indicates who should decide what to do to correct the problem. Now here is a major area in which you do not have to reinvent the wheel. Reference #5 has a five-page summary of corrective actions. Use what you need and add as necessary.

Complete the Corrective Actions column.

HAZARD(S)	CRITICAL CONTROL POINTS (List Only the Operational Steps that are CCPs)	CRITICAL LIMITS	MONITORING	CORRECTIVE ACTIONS	VERIFICATION	R
Salmonella E. Coli O157:H7 C. perfringens Bacillus cereus	CCP – 1 & 3 COOK	155 °F for 15 seconds	Cooking Temp. log @ 30 min. & 1 hr.	Continue cooking until required internal temp. is reached.	Designated HACCP Team member will: Review receiving logs monthly.	Vendor SOPs Food S Manag Thermo c
	CCP – 2 & 5 COOLING	135°F to 70°F within 2 hrs. & 70°F to 41°F within 4 hrs.	Cooling Temp. log @ 2/4/6 hr. intervals	Discard cooked, hot food immediately when the food is: > 70 °F and > 2 hours into the cooling process	Temp. logs weekly Thermometer calibration log weekly Etc…	Tempera Quarter ar au Etc…

Simply put — are you doing what you said you are supposed to be doing? Are you following your plan? If the HACCP Plan says to take the temperature on the serving line every 30 minutes, did the staff do that?

One of the primary tasks of the HACCP team is to ensure the verification is conducted. That verification is done either by a team member or their designated representative. Most importantly, the *"verification should be conducted **by someone other than the person who is directly responsible** for performing the activities specified in the food safety management system."*[3]

References #2 and #3 provide verification activities, frequency and examples listed below. Appendix 11 also provides samples of verification activities.

Verification activities are conducted frequently, such as daily, weekly, monthly, etc., and may include –

- Observing that person(s) are carrying out the critical procedures correctly

- Observing the person doing the monitoring and determining whether monitoring is being done as planned

- Reviewing the monitoring records to determine if they are completed accurately and consistently

- Determining whether the records show that the frequency of monitoring stated in the plan is being followed

- Ensuring that corrective action was taken when the person monitoring found and recorded that the critical limit was not met, as well as documenting what action was taken, by whom and at what time.

- Confirming that all equipment, including equipment used for monitoring, was operated, maintained and calibrated properly

- Sampling of products to see if they meet the specifications, such as observing for dirt in the salad or bones in the meatloaf

Principle 6
Conduct Ongoing Verification

HACCP Principle #6

"Verification includes those activities, other than monitoring, that determine . . . that the system is operating according to the plan."[3]

Frequency of Verification

Verification should occur at a frequency that can ensure the food safety management system is being followed continuously to –

- Prevent unsafe food from reaching the consumer
- Take corrective action without loss of product
- Confirm that prescribed personnel practices are followed
- Ensure that personnel have the tools for proper personal hygiene and sanitary practices (e.g., hand washing facilities, sanitizing equipment, cleaning supplies, temperature measuring devices, etc.)
- Comply with the established control procedures

Complete the Verification column.

HAZARD(S)	CRITICAL CONTROL POINTS (List Only the Operational Steps that are CCPs)	CRITICAL LIMITS	MONITORING	CORRECTIVE ACTIONS	VERIFICATION	RE
Salmonella E. Coli O157:H7 C. perfringens Bacillus cereus	CCP – 1 & 3 COOK	155 °F for 15 seconds	Cooking Temp. log @ 30 min. & 1 hr.	Continue cooking until required internal temp. is reached.	Designated HACCP Team member will: Review receiving logs monthly. Temp. logs weekly Thermometer calibration log weekly Etc...	Vendor SOPs Food Sa Manage Thermol cal Tempera Quarterl anr auc Etc...
	CCP – 2 & 5 COOLING	135°F to 70°F within 2 hrs. & 70°F to 41°F within 4 hrs.	Cooling Temp. log @ 2/4/6 hr. intervals	Discard cooked, hot food immediately when the food is: > 70 °F and > 2 hours into the cooling process		

Listed below are four examples of verification procedures:

➤ **Receiving logs:** Review temperature logs of refrigerated products at various intervals, such as on a weekly basis, or even daily if –

- Receiving a high volume
- Products received include scombroid toxin-forming fish such as fresh tuna.

➤ **Cooling logs:** Check that the "cooling log" is maintained for leftover foods on a weekly basis. The kitchen manager checks to see that the time the food is placed in the cooler, its initial temperature, and measurements of the time and temperature as the food is cooled are recorded and initialed on the log sheet.

➤ **Cooking:** Check the time/temperature monitoring records for cooking nightly to see that the required numbers of temperature measurements were taken during each shift.

Various log samples/templates are provided in References #4 and #5.

Principle 7
Keep Records

HACCP Principle #7

"Records provide documentation that appropriate corrective actions were taken when critical limits were not met. In the event your establishment is implicated in a food-borne illness, documentation of activities related to monitoring and corrective actions can provide proof that reasonable care was exercised in the operation of your establishment. Records may also show that on-going verification was conducted on the food safety management system."[2]

KEEP IT SIMPLE! You want to make sure that it is easy to use and communicate to the employees.

Record keeping systems designed to document your activities are especially useful if you frequently change menu items or products.

Accurately documenting processes like cooking, cooling, and reheating provides a mechanism for ensuring that you have active managerial control of risk factors.

Good records can be your best friend when issues arise. We all know, the piece of information you need is usually the only piece you don't have. The harder it will be to determine what happened, and the more danger that brings, the more records you should keep. So an aircraft carrier and a hospital would keep more records than a yacht and a coffee shop.

There are at least 5 types of records that may be maintained to support your food safety management system:

- Records documenting the activities related to the prerequisite programs
- Monitoring records
- Corrective action records
- Verification and validation records
- Calibration records[3]

Complete the Records column.

HAZARD(S)	CRITICAL CONTROL POINTS (List Only the Operational Steps that are CCPs)	CRITICAL LIMITS	MONITORING	CORRECTIVE ACTIONS	VERIFICATION	RECORDS
Salmonella E. Coli O157:H7 C. perfringens Bacillus cereus	CCP – 1 & 3 COOK	155 °F for 15 seconds	Cooking Temp. log @ 30 min. & 1 hr.	Continue cooking until required internal temp. is reached.	Designated HACCP Team member will: Review receiving logs monthly. Temp. logs weekly Thermometer calibration log weekly Etc...	Vendor Guarantees SOPs Food Safety Checklist Manager Checklist Thermometer calibration log Temperature logs Quarterly, semi-annual & yearly audit sheets Etc...
	CCP – 2 & 5 COOLING	135°F to 70°F within 2 hrs. & 70°F to 41°F within 4 hrs.	Cooling Temp. log @ 2/4/6 hr. intervals	Discard cooked, hot food immediately when the food is: > 70 °F and > 2 hours into the cooling process		

Conclude with completing the Prerequisite Programs area.

PREREQUISITE PROGRAMS	SOPs: Handwashing, Thawing, No Bare Hand contact with RTE, FIFO, etc... Approved source; etc...

The hard work is done!

Yeah right! Now that you have gone through all the principles and established all of the elements listed on **Form A**, all you really have left is to do is break them down into the process or operational steps listed on **Form B** for the appropriate process. See completed form on page 17 and in Appendix 13.

PROCESS STEP	HAZARD(S)	CCPs (Y/N)	CRITICAL LIMITS	MONITORING	CORRECTIVE ACTIONS	VERIFICATION	RECORDS
RECEIVE							
STORE							
PREPARE							
COOK							
COOL							
REHEAT							
HOLD							
SERVE							
PREREQUISITE PROGRAMS							

MENU ITEMS/PRODUCTS:

Conduct Periodic Validation

The bottom line – the plan is effective if people are not getting sick.

"Once your food safety management system is established, you should periodically review it to determine whether the food safety hazards are controlled when the system is implemented properly.

"Changes in suppliers, managers, products, or preparation procedures may prompt a revalidation of your food safety management system. A small change could result in a drastically different outcome from what you expect."[2]

Validation is conducted less frequently (e.g., yearly) than on-going verification. It is a review or audit of the plan to determine if –

- Any new product/processes/menu items have been added to the menu
- Suppliers, customers, equipment, or facilities have changed
- Prerequisite programs are current, documented and implemented
- Worksheets are still current
- CCPs are still valid, or if new CCPs are needed
- Critical Limits are correct in accordance with current regulations (Food Code, county regulations, military manuals, etc.). What is *your* regulatory agency requirement? Does it use the danger zone of 41°-135° or a different one? And are there any scientific articles which might cause us to re-think our procedures, such as evidence regarding the need to re-wash "ready to eat" produce.
- Monitoring equipment has been calibrated as planned[2]
- The incidence of reported foodborne illness is very low as evidenced by checks with local medical, security and/or risk management personnel

Validation helps you to –

- Improve the system and HACCP plan by identifying weaknesses
- Eliminate unnecessary or ineffective controls
- Determine if the HACCP plan needs to be modified or updated[2]
- Determine if the plan is EFFECTIVE in that people are not getting sick

A sample validation worksheet[2] has been included here as Appendix 12.

At last . . .

Now you have your Masterpiece! Don't be lulled into thinking that you are done. *"What!?"* you say. Your masterpiece is a LIVING document that will change periodically as menus or processes change. Even the change of management could impact the processes in use. In fact any time there is a change in management, it would be an ideal time to review and update your documented plan – your Masterpiece. The creation of a documented plan is only the beginning. The team must ensure the implementation is carried out and maintained.

Appendix 13 provides you with the completed sample of the process #3 item that we used throughout the manual. Keep in mind that it is NOT an all inclusive sample. Additionally, the author created a modified version of the forms used in the manual. Appendix 14 provides you with an alternative format for documenting your HACCP plan.

Once your team has gone through the whole process once, it won't seem to be as daunting a task as you review and update your plan.

As you can see, there is a logical process for documenting your HACCP plan. It is said, "The best way to eat an elephant is one bite at a time." So don't rush yourselves, take the time to go through each step. The more times you go through the process the more familiar and easy it gets. You will find that many items are repetitive in nature with regards to hazards, critical control points, critical limits, and even monitoring.

I am sure by now you can see that because of all the variations from one facility to another that there could not be a single "all inclusive" book. I would dare to say that in working through the samples you have said to yourself – at least once – we don't do it that way... and you are right. There are hundreds of ways to prepare an item, just make sure you are documenting it and doing it safely.

Your comments will help us to improve later editions. We hope you enjoy using it as much as we enjoyed putting it together. Have fun with the great learning experience of putting together a HACCP program, and take pride in the work you are doing on behalf of your customers.

> Your masterpiece is a LIVING document that will change periodically as menus, products or processes change.

> Questions, comments, kudos and suggestions can be sent to Ann or Ed at Ed@EHManley.com or visit our website at www.EHManley.com

Appendices

On the next three pages are two examples of a SOP regarding Receiving. The first is a sample from Alaska's AMC computer program. The second is from the National Food Service Management Institute (NFSMI). Both are used with permissions from the organizations.

Don't let semantics get in the way. Mix and match – customize to YOUR facility. The point here is that there are samples that you can use; you DO NOT have to recreate the wheel. There may be some instances where your facility is so different that you will have to add some verbiage to make it specific to you.

Appendix 1

Developing SOPs

Header Topics used by automated AMC program	Header Topics used by NFSMI
Why:	Purpose:
Who:	Scope:
When:	Key Words:
Where:	Instructions:
How:	Monitoring:
Mandatory Records: (if applicable)	Corrective Action:
Optional Records	Verification and Record Keeping:
Correction:	Correction:
PIC Verification:	Date implementation:

PIC= Person in Charge

Standard Operating Procedures for

Facility Name: _____

Handwashing

Why:	Unclean hands can transfer bacteria and viruses to food, and cross-contaminate foods and food contact surfaces.
Who:	All food workers.

When: Food handlers must wash their hands:
- Before starting work.
- Before putting on or changing gloves.
- After using the restroom, (use the restroom sink).
- After touching their hair, face or body.
- After eating, drinking, smoking, or touching chewing gum.
- Upon entering a food prep area.
- After cleaning or taking out the garbage.
- After touching anything that contaminates the hands.
- After using chemicals.
- ☐ _____

Where: Only at the designated handwashing or restroom sink.

How:
1. Use warm water (greater than 100° less than 120°)
2. Wet hands and exposed arms up to the elbow
3. Apply hand soap
4. Rub hands and forearms vigorously for 20 seconds
5. Clean under fingernails
6. Rinse under warm water
7. Towel dry with disposable towels
8. Be careful not to re-contaminate hands on faucets, paper towel dispenser, or door handle.
- ☐ _____

Correction: • Observe employee handwashing practices and instruct them to rewash their hands if not washed properly.
• Retrain employee in proper handwashing procedures.
- ☐ _____

**PIC
Verification:**   Check that:
- Soap and paper towels are available.
- Sinks are accessible and conveniently located.
- Water temperature and pressure are adequate.
- Employees are following this SOP.
- ☐ Handwashing signs are posted demonstrating proper handwashing steps.
- ☐ _____

Prepared or revised by:

Signature: _____Date_____

**Alaska Food Safety and Sanitation Program "Standard Operating Procedure" Template
www.state.ak.us/dec/eh**

HACCP-Based SOPs

Washing Hands (Sample SOP)

**Sample 2. SOP –
National Food
Service Management
Institute program**

Used with permission

PURPOSE: To prevent foodborne illness by contaminated hands.

SCOPE: This procedure applies to anyone who handle, prepare, and serve food.

KEY WORDS: Handwashing, Cross-Contamination

INSTRUCTIONS:
1. Train foodservice employees on using the procedures in this SOP.
2. Follow State or local health department requirements.
3. Post handwashing signs or posters in a language understood by all food service staff near all handwashing sinks, in food preparation areas, and restrooms.
4. Use designated handwashing sinks for handwashing only. Do not use food preparation, utility, and dishwashing sinks for handwashing.
5. Provide warm running water, soap, and a means to dry hands. Provide a waste container at each handwashing sink or near the door in restrooms.
6. Keep handwashing sinks accessible anytime employees are present.
7. Wash hands:
   - Before starting work
   - During food preparation
   - When moving from one food preparation area to another
   - Before putting on or changing gloves
   - After using the toilet
   - After sneezing, coughing, or using a handkerchief or tissue
   - After touching hair, face, or body
   - After smoking, eating, drinking, or chewing gum or tobacco
   - After handling raw meats, poultry, or fish
   - After any clean up activity such as sweeping, mopping, or wiping counters
   - After touching dirty dishes, equipment, or utensils
   - After handling trash
   - After handling money
   - After any time the hands may become contaminated
8. Follow proper handwashing procedures as indicated below:
   - Wet hands and forearms with warm, running water at least 100 °F and apply soap.
   - Scrub lathered hands and forearms, under fingernails, and between fingers for at least 10-15 seconds. Rinse thoroughly under warm running water for 5-10 seconds.
   - Dry hands and forearms thoroughly with single-use paper towels.
   - Dry hands for at least 30 seconds if using a warm air hand dryer.
   - Turn off water using paper towels.
   - Use paper towel to open door when exiting the restroom.
9. Follow FDA recommendations when using hand sanitizers. These recommendations are as follows:
   - Use hand sanitizers only after hands have been properly washed and dried.
   - Use only hand sanitizers that comply with the *2001 FDA Food Code*.
   - Confirm with the manufacturers that the hand sanitizers used meet these requirements.
   - Use hand sanitizers in the manner specified by the manufacturer.

Continued on next page

HACCP-Based SOPs

Washing Hands, continued
(Sample SOP)

MONITORING:
1. A designated employee will visually observe the handwashing practices of the foodservice staff during all hours of operation.
2. The designated employee will visually observe that handwashing sinks are properly supplied during all hours of operation.

CORRECTIVE ACTION:
1. Retrain any foodservice employee found not following the procedures in this SOP.
2. Ask employees that are observed not washing their hands at the appropriate times or using the proper procedure to wash their hands immediately.
3. Retrain employee to ensure proper handwashing procedure.

VERIFICATION AND RECORD KEEPING:
The foodservice manager will complete the Food Safety Checklist daily to indicate that monitoring is being conducted as specified. The Food Safety Checklist is to be kept on file for a minimum of 1 year.

DATE IMPLEMENTED: _____   BY: _____

DATE REVIEWED: _____   BY: _____

DATE REVISED: _____   BY: _____

Form 1A
Process #1 – Food Preparation with No Cook Step

MENU ITEMS/PRODUCTS:

HAZARDS	CRITICAL CONTROL POINTS (List Only the Operational Steps that are CCPs)	CRITICAL LIMITS	MONITORING	CORRECTIVE ACTIONS	VERIFICATION	RECORDS

PREREQUISITE PROGRAMS

(Source: Managing Food Safety: A Manual for the Voluntary Use of HACCP Principles for Operators of Food Service and Retail Establishments)

Form 1B

Process #1 – Food Preparation with No Cook Step

MENU ITEMS/PRODUCTS:

PROCESS STEP	HAZARD(S)	CCPs (Y/N)	CRITICAL LIMITS	MONITORING	CORRECTIVE ACTIONS	VERIFICATION	RECORDS
RECEIVE							
STORE							
PREPARE							
HOLD							
SERVE							
PREREQUISITE PROGRAMS							

(Source: Managing Food Safety: A Manual for the Voluntary Use of HACCP Principles for Operators of Food Service and Retail Establishments)

Form 2A

Process #2 – Preparation for Same Day Service

MENU ITEMS/PRODUCTS:

HAZARDS	CRITICAL CONTROL POINTS (List Only the Operational Steps that are CCPs)	CRITICAL LIMITS	MONITORING	CORRECTIVE ACTIONS	VERIFICATION	RECORDS

PREREQUISITE PROGRAMS	

(Source: Managing Food Safety: A Manual for the Voluntary Use of HACCP Principles for Operators of Food Service and Retail Establishments)

Form 2B
Process #2 – Preparation for Same Day Service

MENU ITEMS/PRODUCTS:

PROCESS STEP	HAZARD(S)	CCPs (Y/N)	CRITICAL LIMITS	MONITORING	CORRECTIVE ACTIONS	VERIFICATION	RECORDS
RECEIVE							
STORE							
PREPARE							
COOK							
HOLD							
SERVE							
PREREQUISITE PROGRAMS							

(Source: Managing Food Safety: A Manual for the Voluntary Use of HACCP Principles for Operators of Food Service and Retail Establishments)

Form 3A
Process #3 – Complex Food Preparation

MENU ITEMS/PRODUCTS:

HAZARDS	CRITICAL CONTROL POINTS (List Only the Operational Steps that are CCPs)	CRITICAL LIMITS	MONITORING	CORRECTIVE ACTIONS	VERIFICATION	RECORDS
PREREQUISITE PROGRAMS						

(Source: Managing Food Safety: A Manual for the Voluntary Use of HACCP Principles for Operators of Food Service and Retail Establishments)

Form 3B
Process #3 – Complex Food Preparation

MENU ITEMS/PRODUCTS:

PROCESS STEP	HAZARD(S)	CCPs (Y/N)	CRITICAL LIMITS	MONITORING	CORRECTIVE ACTIONS	VERIFICATION	RECORDS
RECIEVE							
STORE							
PREPARE							
COOK							
COOL							
REHEAT							
HOLD							
SERVE							
PREREQUISITE PROGRAMS							

(Source: Managing Food Safety: A Manual for the Voluntary Use of HACCP Principles for Operators of Food Service and Retail Establishments)

	HAZARD	ASSOCIATED FOODS	CONTROL MEASURES
Bacteria	*Bacillus cereus* (intoxication caused by heat-stable, preformed emetic toxin or toxicoinfection caused by heat-labile, diarrheal toxin)	Meat, poultry, starchy foods (rice, potatoes), puddings, soups, cooked vegetables	Cooking, Cooling, Cold Holding, Hot Holding
	Campylobacter jejuni	Poultry, raw milk	Cooking, Handwashing, Prevention of Cross-contamination
	Clostridium botulinum (intoxication caused by preformed heat-labile toxin)	Vacuum-packed foods, reduced oxygen packaged foods, under-processed canned foods, garlic-in-oil mixtures, time/temperature abused baked potatoes/sautéed onions	Thermal Processing (Time + Pressure), Cooling, Cold Holding, Hot Holding, Acidification and Drying, etc.
	Clostridium perfringens	Cooked meat and poultry, Cooked meat and poultry products including casseroles, gravies	Cooling, Cold Holding, Reheating, Hot Holding
	E. coli O157:H7 (other shiga toxin-producing *E. coli*)	Raw ground beef, raw seed sprouts, raw milk, unpasteurized juice, foods contaminated by infected food workers via fecal-oral route	Cooking, No Bare Hand Contact with RTE Foods, Employee Health Policy, Handwashing, Prevention of Cross-contamination, Pasteurization or Treatment of Juice
	Listeria monocytogenes	Raw meat and poultry, fresh soft cheese, Pate, smoked seafood, deli meats, deli salads	Cooking, Date Marking, Cold Holding, Handwashing, Prevention of Cross-contamination
	Salmonella spp.	Meat and poultry, seafood, eggs, raw seed sprouts, raw vegetables, raw milk, unpasteurized juice	Cooking, Use of Pasteurized Eggs, Employee Health Policy, No Bare Hand Contact with RTE foods, Handwashing, Pasteurization or Treatment of Juice
	Shigella spp.	Raw vegetables and herbs, other foods contaminated by infected workers via fecal-oral route	Cooking, No Bare Hand Contact with RTE Foods, Employee Health Policy, Handwashing
	Staphylococcus aureus (intoxication caused by preformed heat-stable toxin)	RTE PHFs touched by bare hands after cooking and further time/temperature abused	Cooling, Cold Holding, Hot Holding, No Bare Hand Contact with RTE Food, Handwashing
	Vibrio spp.	Seafood, shellfish	Cooking, Approved Source, Prevention of Cross-contamination
Parasites	*Anisakis simplex*	Various fish (cod, haddock, fluke, pacific salmon, herring, flounder, monkfish)	Cooking, Freezing
	Taenia spp.	Beef and pork	Cooking
	Trichinella spiralis	Pork, bear and seal meat	Cooking
Viruses	Hepatitis A and E	Shellfish, any food contaminated by infected worker via fecal-oral route	Approved Source, No Bare Hand Contact with RTE Food, Minimizing Bare Hand Contact with Foods Not RTE, Employee Health Policy, Handwashing
	Other Viruses (Rotaviruses, Noroviruses, Reoviruses)	Any food contaminated by infected worker via fecal-oral route	No Bare Hand Contact with RTE Food, Minimizing Bare Hand Contact with Foods Not RTE, Employee Health Policy, Handwashing

(Source: Managing Food Safety: A Manual for the Voluntary Use of HACCP Principles for Operators of Food Service and Retail Establishments)

Appendix 4   Natural Toxins[1] in Seafood

Natural Toxins	Type of fish (species)	Control
Paralytic Shellfish Poisoning (PSP)	Molluscan Shellfish N.E. and N.W. coastal regions of N. America	NSSP approved waters (tags)[2] (FDA ICSSL listing)
Neurotoxic Shellfish Poisoning (NSP)	Molluscan Shellfish harvested along coast of Gulf of Mexico	NSSP approved waters (tags)[2] (FDA ICSSL listing)
Diarrhetic Shellfish Poisoning (DSP)	Molluscan Shellfish	NSSP approved waters (tags)[2] (FDA ICSSL listing)
Amnesic Shellfish Poisoning (ASP)	Molluscan Shellfish N.E. & N.W. coasts of N. America	NSSP approved waters (tags)[2] (FDA ICSSL listing)
Ciguatera Fish Poisoning (CFP)	fin fish from extreme S.E. U.S., Hawaii, Subtropical and Tropical areas: barracuda amberjack horse-eye jack black jack other larger species of jack king mackerel large groupers large snappers	Purchase from approved sources: • get fish from areas that are not subject of an adverse advisory, or • get fish from a reef area known to be monitored for toxicity and not covered by an adverse advisory.
Gempylotoxin, a strong purgative oil (can cause severe diarrhea)	Escolar	FDA recommendation: Escolar should not be marketed in interstate commerce
Etrodotoxin	Puffer Fish or Fugu, usually from Indo-Pacific ocean, however some noted from Atlantic Ocean, Gulf of Mexico and Gulf of California	Illegal to import or receive (exemption: an agreement with one N.Y. importer)

1 Fish and Fishery Products Hazards and Controls Guide, Third Edition, June 2001
2The tags must contain a unique state issued "certification number" specific for each certified dealer. If the firm is engaged in interstate commerce, this number appears in FDA's Interstate Certified Shellfish Shippers List.

(Source: Managing Food Safety: A Manual for the Voluntary Use of HACCP Principles for Operators of Food Service and Retail Establishments)

Toxin Formation	Species - Market Names	Control
Scombrotoxin formation as a result of time/temperature abuse	Most scombroid poisonings from tuna, mahi-mahi and bluefish. Other species are: Amberjack or yellowtail Anchovy Bluefish Bonito Escolar or Snake Mackerel Gemfish Herring (not River herring) Jack Jobfish Kahawai Mackerel (not Atka) Mahi-Mahi Marlin Pilchard or Sardine Sardine Saury Shad & roe Shad, Gizzard Snapper (Pristipomoides ssp) Sprat or Bristling Trevally Tuna Wahoo	* Buy from approved federally inspected suppliers. They are required to receive, hold, and process using a HACCP system. * Check for an adequate quantity of ice or other cooling media. * If not, a federally inspected supplier or directly from a fishing boat, check for the following at receipt: - an adequate quantity of ice or other cooling media - the time the fish were caught (from the vessel or supplier) - See * information below

[1] Fish and Fishery Products Hazards and Controls Guide, Third Edition, June 2001

- <u>FDA Recommended HACCP Controls for Histamine – Quick reference</u>

Secondary Processor (Controls at receipt)

Transport records
OR
(< 40 °F throughout transit)

Adequate Ice/cooling media

surrounding product at delivery

Processing/ Storage

Fresh (not previously frozen)		Previously frozen	
≤4 hrs @ > 40 °F if any exposure is > 70 °F	≤8 hrs @ > 40 °F if NO exposure is > 70 °F	≤12 hrs @ > 40 °F if any exposure is > 70 °F	≤24 hrs @ > 40 °F if NO exposure is > 70 °F

(Source: Managing Food Safety: A Manual for the Voluntary Use of HACCP Principles for Operators of Food Service and Retail Establishments)

Appendix 6   Common Parasites in Seafood[1]

Parasites[2]	Type of fish/species likely to be used in menu items that will not be cooked		Control
Nematodes or roundworm Cestodes or tapeworms Trematodes or flukes	Sea bass Capelin & roe Cod Flounder - Dab - Fluke Grouper Halibut Herring Jack Jobfish Kahawai Mackerel Monkfish Mullet	Chilean Sea Bass Ocean Perch Plaice Pollock Rockfish Sablefish Salmon & roe (aquacultured & wild) Seatrout Sole Sprat/Bristling Trout/steelhead/rainbow Tuna, small Turbot Wolfish	Purchase from a processor, require the raw fish to have been: • Frozen and stored at -4 °F (-20 °C) or below for 7 days; or • Frozen at -31 °F (-35 °C) or below and stored at -31 °F (-35 °C) for 15 hours; or • Frozen at -31 °F (-35 °C) or below until solid and stored at -4 °F (-20 °C) for 24 hrs. Freezing can be done in your operation if it is done in accordance with the Food Code, Chapter 3.

[1]Fish and Fishery Products Hazards and Controls Guide, Third Edition, June 2001

[2]Some food products that have been implicated in human parasitic infection are:

ceviche	salmon roe	green herring	undercooked grilled fish
lomi lomi	sashimi	drunken crabs	
poisson cru	sushi	cold smoke fish	

(Source: Managing Food Safety: A Manual for the Voluntary Use of HACCP Principles for Operators of Food Service and Retail Establishments)

HACCP Implementation – a Quick Reference Manual

Chemical Hazards	Associated Foods	Control measures
Naturally Occurring:		
Scombrotoxin	Primarily associated with tuna fish, mahi-mahi, blue fish, anchovies bonito, mackerel; Also found in cheese	Check temperatures at receiving; store at proper cold holding temperatures; buyer specifications: obtain verification from supplier that product has not been temperature abused prior to arrival in facility.
Ciguatoxin	Reef fin fish from extreme SE US, Hawaii, and tropical areas; barracuda, jacks, king mackerel, large groupers, and snappers	Ensure fin fish have not been caught: • Purchase fish from approved sources. • Fish should not be harvested from an area that is subject to an adverse advisory.
Tetrodoxin	Puffer fish (Fugu; Blowfish)	Do not consume these fish.
Mycotoxins Aflatoxin Patulin	 Corn and corn products, peanuts and peanut products, cottonseed, milk, and tree nuts such as Brazil nuts, pecans, pistachio nuts, and walnuts. Other grains and nuts are susceptible but less prone to contamination. Apple juice products	 Check condition at receiving; do not use moldy or decomposed food. Buyer Specification: obtain verification from supplier or avoid the use of rotten apples in juice manufacturing.
Toxic mushroom species	Numerous varieties of wild mushrooms	Do not eat unknown varieties or mushrooms from unapproved source.
Shellfish toxins Paralytic shellfish poisoning (PSP) Diarrhetic shellfish poisoning (DSP) Neurotoxin shellfish poisoning (NSP) Amnesic shellfish poisoning (ASP)	Molluscan shellfish from NE and NW coastal regions; mackerel, viscera of lobsters and Dungeness, tanner, and red rock crabs Molluscan shellfish in Japan, western Europe, Chile, NZ, eastern Canada Molluscan shellfish from Gulf of Mexico Molluscan shellfish from NE and NW coasts of NA; viscera of Dungeness, tanner, red rock crabs and anchovies.	Ensure molluscan shellfish are: • from an approved source; and • properly tagged and labeled.
Pyrrolizidine alkaloids	Plants food containing these alkaloids. Most commonly found in members of the Borginaceae, Compositae, and Leguminosae families.	Do not consume of food or medicinals contaminated with these alkaloids.
Phtyohaemmagglutinin	Raw red kidney beans (Undercooked beans may be more toxic than raw beans)	Soak in water for at least 5 hours. Pour away the water. Boil briskly in fresh water, with occasional stirring, for at least 10 minutes

(Source: Annex 4 – Management of Food Safety Practices – Achieving Active Managerial Control of Foodborne Illness Risk Factors)

Continued on next page

Appendix 7

Continued

Chemical Hazards	Associated Foods	Control measures
Added Chemicals:		
Environmental contaminants: Pesticides, fungicides, fertilizers, insecticides, antibiotics, growth hormones	Any food may become contaminated.	Follow label instructions for use of environmental chemicals. Soil or water analysis may be used to verify safety.
PCBs	Fish	Comply with fish advisories.
Prohibited substances (21 CFR 189)	Numerous substances are prohibited from use in human food; no substance may be used in human food unless it meets all applicable requirements of the FD&C Act.	Do not use chemical substances that are not approved for use in human food.
Toxic elements/compounds Mercury	Fish exposed to organic mercury: shark, tilefish, king mackerel and swordfish. Grains treated with mercury based fungicides	Pregnant women/women of childbearing age/nursing mothers, and young children should not eat shark, swordfish, king mackerel or tilefish because they contain high levels of mercury. Do not use mercury containing fungicides on grains or animals.
Copper	High acid foods and beverages	Do not store high acid foods in copper utensils; use backflow prevention device on beverage vending machines.
Lead	High acid food and beverages	Do not use vessels containing lead.
Preservatives and Food Additives: Sulfiting agents (sulfur dioxide, sodium and potassium bisulfite, sodium and potassium metabisulfite)	Fresh fruits and Vegetables Shrimp Lobster Wine	Sulfiting agents added to a product in a processing plant must be declared on labeling. Do not use on raw produce in food establishments.
Naturally Occurring:		
Nitrites/nitrates Niacin	Cured meats, fish, any food exposed to accidental contamination, spinach Meat and other foods to which sodium nicotinate is added	Do not use more than the prescribed amount of curing compound according to labeling instructions. Sodium nicotinate (niacin) is not currently approved for use in meat or poultry with or without nitrates or nitrates.
Flavor enhancers Monosodium glutamate (MSG)	Asian or Latin American food	Avoid using excessive amounts
Chemicals used in retail establishments (e.g., lubricants, cleaners, sanitizers, cleaning compounds, and paints	Any food could become contaminated	Address through SOPs for proper labeling, storage, handling, and use of chemicals; retain Material Safety Data Sheets for all chemicals.
Allergens	Foods containing or contacted by: Milk Egg Fish Crustacean shellfish Tree nuts Wheat Peanuts Soybeans	Use a rigorous sanitation regime to prevent cross contact between allergenic and non-allergenic ingredients.

(Source: Annex 4 – Management of Food Safety Practices — Achieving Active Managerial Control of Foodborne Illness Risk Factors)

Main Materials of Concern as Physical Hazards and Common Sources[a, b]

Material	Injury Potential	Sources
Glass fixtures	Cuts, bleeding; may require surgery to find or remove	Bottles, jars, lights, utensils, gauge covers
Wood	Cuts, infection, choking; may require surgery to remove	Fields, pallets, boxes, buildings
Stones, metal fragments	Choking, broken teeth Cuts, infection; may require surgery to remove	Fields, buildings, machinery, wire, employees
Insulation	Choking; long-term if asbestos	Building materials
Bone	Choking, trauma	Fields, improper plant processing
Plastic	Choking, cuts, infection; may require surgery to remove	Fields, plant packaging materials, pallets, employees
Personal effects	Choking, cuts, broken teeth; may require surgery to remove	Employees

[a] Adapted from Corlett (1991).
[b] Used with permission, "HACCP Principles and Applications", Pierson and Corlett, Eds. 1992. Chapman & Hall, New York, NY.

(Source: Annex 4 – Management of Food Safety Practices – Achieving Active Managerial Control of Foodborne Illness Risk Factors)

 **Appendix 9**   **Foods That Might Be Served Raw or Undercooked**

Raw Animal Food	Menu Items	Hazards
Beef	Steak Tartare Carpaccio	*Salmonella spp.* *Escherichia coli* 0157:H7
Poultry	Duck	*Salmonella spp.* *Campylobacter jejuni*
Eggs	Quiche, hollandaise sauce, Eggs Benedict, homemade mayonnaise, meringue pie, some puddings and custards, Monte Cristo sandwich, mousse, tiramisu, chicken croquettes, rice balls, stuffing, lasagna, french toast, crab cakes, egg nog, fish stuffing, Caesar salad, ice cream	*Salmonella* Enteritidis
Raw Fish/Finfish	Lightly cooked fish, sushi, raw-marinated, cold-smoked fish, ceviche, tuna carpaccio	*Anisakis simplex* *Diphyllobothrium*spp. *Pseudoterranova decipiens* *Vibrio parahaemolyticus*
	Reef fish: (barracuda, amberjack, horse-eye jack, black/jack, other large species of jack, king mackerel, large groupers, large snappers)	Ciguatera toxin
Shellfish	Oysters Clams	*Vibrio vulnificus* *Vibrio* spp. Hepatitis A Norovirus
Raw Dairy Products	Raw or unpasteurized milk, some soft cheeses like Camembert, Brie, etc.	*Listeria monocytogenes* *Salmonella spp.* *Campylobacter jejuni* *E. coli* O157:H7

(Source: Managing Food Safety: A Manual for the Voluntary Use of HACCP Principles for Operators of Food Service and Retail Establishments)

Appendix 10

(Source: Hazard Analysis and Critical Control Point Principles and Application Guidelines, Aug 1997)

The hazard analysis consists of asking a series of questions which are appropriate to the process under consideration. The purpose of the questions is to assist in identifying potential hazards.

A. Ingredients
1. Does the food contain any sensitive ingredients that may present microbiological hazards (e.g., Salmonella, Staphylococcus aureus); chemical hazards (e.g., aflatoxin, antibiotic or pesticide residues); or physical hazards (stones, glass, metal)?
2. Are potable water, ice and steam used in formulating or in handling the food?
3. What are the sources (e.g., geographical region, specific supplier)

B. Intrinsic Factors - Physical characteristics and composition (e.g., pH, type of acidulants, fermentable carbohydrate, water activity, preservatives) of the food during and after processing.
1. What hazards may result if the food composition is not controlled?
2. Does the food permit survival or multiplication of pathogens and/or toxin formation in the food during processing?
3. Will the food permit survival or multiplication of pathogens and/or toxin formation during subsequent steps in the food chain?
4. Are there other similar products in the market place? What has been the safety record for these products? What hazards have been associated with the products?

C. Procedures used for processing
1. Does the process include a controllable processing step that destroys pathogens? If so, which pathogens? Consider both vegetative cells and spores.
2. If the product is subject to recontamination between processing (e.g., cooking, pasteurizing) and packaging which biological, chemical or physical hazards are likely to occur?

D. Microbial content of the food
1. What is the normal microbial content of the food?
2. Does the microbial population change during the normal time the food is stored prior to consumption?
3. Does the subsequent change in microbial population alter the safety of the food?
4. Do the answers to the above questions indicate a high likelihood of certain biological hazards?

E. Facility design
1. Does the layout of the facility provide an adequate separation of raw materials from ready-to-eat (RTE) foods if this is important to food safety? If not, what hazards should be considered as possible contaminants of the RTE products?
2. Is positive air pressure maintained in product packaging areas? Is this essential for product safety?
3. Is the traffic pattern for people and moving equipment a significant source of contamination?

F. Equipment design and use
1. Will the equipment provide the time-temperature control that is necessary for safe food?
2. Is the equipment properly sized for the volume of food that will be processed?
3. Can the equipment be sufficiently controlled so that the variation in performance will be within the tolerances required to produce a safe food?
4. Is the equipment reliable or is it prone to frequent breakdowns?
5. Is the equipment designed so that it can be easily cleaned and sanitized?
6. Is there a chance for product contamination with hazardous substances; e.g., glass?

7. What product safety devices are used to enhance consumer safety?
   - metal detectors
   - sifters
   - screens
   - bone removal devices
   - magnets
   - filters
   - thermometers
   - dud detectors
8. To what degree will normal equipment wear affect the likely occurrence of a physical hazard (e.g., metal) in the product?
9. Are allergen protocols needed in using equipment for different products?

G. Packaging
1. Does the method of packaging affect the multiplication of microbial pathogens and/or the formation of toxins?
2. Is the package clearly labeled "Keep Refrigerated" if this is required for safety?
3. Does the package include instructions for the safe handling and preparation of the food by the end user?
4. Is the packaging material resistant to damage thereby preventing the entrance of microbial contamination?
5. Are tamper-evident packaging features used?
6. Is each package and case legibly and accurately coded?
7. Does each package contain the proper label?
8. Are potential allergens in the ingredients included in the list of ingredients on the label?

H. Sanitation
1. Can sanitation have an impact upon the safety of the food that is being processed?
2. Can the facility and equipment be easily cleaned and sanitized to permit the safe handling of food?
3. Is it possible to provide sanitary conditions consistently and adequately to assure safe foods?

I. Employee health, hygiene and education
1. Can employee health or personal hygiene practices impact upon the safety of the food being processed?
2. Do the employees understand the process and the factors they must control to assure the preparation of safe foods?
3. Will the employees inform management of a problem which could impact upon safety of food?

J. Conditions of storage between packaging and the end user
1. What is the likelihood that the food will be improperly stored at the wrong temperature?
2. Would an error in improper storage lead to a microbiologically unsafe food?

K. Intended use
1. Will the food be heated by the consumer?
2. Will there likely be leftovers?

L. Intended consumer
1. Is the food intended for the general public?
2. Is the food intended for consumption by a population with increased susceptibility to illness (e.g., infants, the aged, the infirmed, immuno-compromised individuals)?
3. Is the food to be used for institutional feeding or the home?

A. Verification procedures may include:
1. Establishment of appropriate verification schedules.
2. Review of the HACCP plan for completeness.
3. Confirmation of the accuracy of the flow diagram.
4. Review of the HACCP system to determine if the facility is operating according to the HACCP plan.
5. Review of CCP monitoring records.
6. Review of records for deviations and corrective actions.
7. Validation of critical limits to confirm that they are adequate to control significant hazards.
8. Validation of HACCP plan, including on-site review.
9. Review of modifications of the HACCP plan.
10. Sampling and testing to verify CCPs.

B. Verification should be conducted:
1. Routinely, or on an unannounced basis, to assure CCPs are under control.
2. When there are emerging concerns about the safety of the product.
3. When foods have been implicated as a vehicle of food-borne disease.
4. To confirm that changes have been implemented correctly after a HACCP plan has been modified.
5. To assess whether a HACCP plan should be modified due to a change in the process, equipment, ingredients, etc.

C. Verification reports may include information on the presence and adequacy of.
1. The HACCP plan and the person(s) responsible for administering and updating the HACCP plan.
2. The records associated with CCP monitoring.
3. Direct recording of monitoring data of the CCP while in operation.
4. Certification that monitoring equipment is properly calibrated and in working order.
5. Corrective actions for deviations.
6. Sampling and testing methods used to verify that CCPs are under control.
7. Modifications to the HACCP plan.
8. Training and knowledge of individuals responsible for monitoring CCPs.
9. Validation activities.

Appendix 12　Validation Worksheet

Date: _____ 　　Date of last validation: 　　_____

_____　　　　　　_____
Name of person responsible for validation: 　　　　　　　　　　　　Title:

Frequency at which the validation is done: 　Quarterly ☐ 　Yearly ☐ 　Other: _____

The length of time this record is kept on file (i.e. # months or years): 　　_____

Reason, other than frequency, for 　　_____
doing the validation: 　　　　　　　_____

1.
(a) Has a new product, process, or menu item been added since the last validation? 　Yes ☐ Go to Q #1b 　No ☐

(b) Has the supplier, customer, equipment, or facility changed since the last validation? 　Yes ☐ 　No ☐ Go to Q #2

2. Are the existing worksheets accurate and current? 　Yes ☐ Go to Q #3 　No ☐ Worksheet Info updated:
Date: _____
By: _____

3. Are the identified hazards accurate and current? 　Yes ☐ Go to Q #4 　No ☐ Hazard analysis updated:
Date: _____
By: _____

4. Are the existing CCPs correctly identified? 　Yes ☐ Go to Q #5 　No ☐ CCPs updated:
Date: _____
By: _____

5. Are the existing critical limits appropriate to control each hazard? 　Yes ☐ Go to Q #6 　No ☐ CLs updated:
Date: _____
By: _____

6. Do the existing monitoring procedures ensure that the critical limits are met? 　Yes ☐ Go to Q #7 　No ☐ Monitoring procedures updated:
Date: _____
By: _____

7. Do existing corrective actions ensure that no injurious food is served or purchased? 　Yes ☐ Go to Q #8 　No ☐ Corrective Actions updated:
Date: _____
By: _____

8. Do the existing on-going verification procedures ensure that the food safety and is consistently followed? 　Yes ☐ Go to Q #9 　No ☐ On-going verification procedures updated:
Date: _____
By: _____

9. Does the existing record keeping system provide adequate documentation that the critical limits are met and corrective actions are taken when needed? 　Yes ☐ Go to Q #10 　No ☐ Record keeping procedures updated:
Date: _____
By: _____

10. Is the incidence of reported foodborne illness complaints at an acceptable level? 　Yes ☐ 　No ☐ Verified plan for discrepencies:
Date: _____
By: _____

➲ The validation procedure is now complete. The next validation is due _____ .
➲ The changes made to the food safety management system
were conveyed to the line supervisor or front-line employees on _____ .

Completed by: Name _____

Title _____

Form 3A
Process #3 – Complex Food Preparation

MENU ITEMS/PRODUCTS:
Lasagna, Taco meat, tamales, etc..

HAZARD(S)	CRITICAL CONTROL POINTS (List Only the Operational Steps that are CCPs)	CRITICAL LIMITS	MONITORING	CORRECTIVE ACTIONS	VERIFICATION	RECORDS
Salmonella E. Coli O157:H7 C. perfringens Bacillus cereus	CCP – 1 & 3 COOK	155 °F for 15 seconds	Cooking Temp. log @ 30 min. & 1 hr.	Continue cooking until required internal temp. is reached.	Designated HACCP Team member will: Review receiving logs monthly. Temp. logs weekly Thermometer calibration log weekly Etc....	Vendor Guarantees SOPs Food Safety Checklist Manager Checklist Thermometer calibration log Temperature logs Quarterly, semi-annual & yearly audit sheets Etc....
	CCP – 2 & 5 COOLING	135°F to 70°F within 2 hrs. & 70°F to 41°F within 4 hrs.	Cooling Temp. log @ 2/4/6 hr. intervals	Discard cooked, hot food immediately when the food is > 70 °F and > 2 hours into the cooling process		
	CCP – 4 HOT HOLDING	135°F or higher	Hot Holding Temp. log @ 1 hr. intervals	Reheat to 165 °F for 15 sec. if temp. is <135 °F and was >135 °F or higher within the last 2 hours.		
	CCP – 6 COLD HOLDING	41°F or below	Cold Holding Temp. log @ 1 hr. intervals	Discard food if can't determine how long the food temp. was >41 °F.		
	CCP – 7 REHEATING	165°F for 15 seconds	Reheating log	Continue cooking until required internal temp. is reached.		
PREREQUISITE PROGRAMS	SOPs: Handwashing, Thawing, No Bare Hand contact with RTE, FIFO, etc... Approved source; etc....					

Form 3B
Process #3 – Complex Food Preparation
MENU ITEMS/PRODUCTS:
Lasagna, Taco meat, tamales, etc.

PROCESS STEP	HAZARD(S)	CCPs (Y/N)	CRITICAL LIMITS	MONITORING	CORRECTIVE ACTIONS	VERIFICATION	RECORDS
RECEIVE	Salmonella E. Coli O 157:H7 C. perfingens Bacillus cereus	N #	Approved source Shellfish tags	Vendor agreement Receiving logs	Refuse product	(who) review logs weekly , verify supplies monthly	*Vendor Guarantees *SOPs
STORE		Y	Cold - <41ºF RTE above raw FIFO	Refrigerator logs Observation	Report high refrigerator temps to Engineering	(who) review logs weekly, verifies stock rotation	*Food Safety Checklist *Manager Checklist
PREPARE		Y ##	Thaw in cooler/under running water, no bare hand contact with RTE	Observation	Retain employees	(who) review incident logs or training records	*Thermometer calibration log
COOK		Y	155 ºF for 15 seconds	Cooking Temp. log @30 min. & 1 hr.	Continue cooking until required internal temp. is reached.	(who) review logs weekly	*Temperature logs *Quarterly, semi-annual & yearly audit sheets Etc...
COOL		Y	135ºF to 70ºF within 2 hrs. & 70ºF to 41ºF within 4 hrs.	Cooling Temp. log @ 2/4/6 hr. intervals	Discard cooked, hot food immediately when the food is: > 70 ºF and > 2 hours into the cooling process	(who) review logs weekly	
REHEAT		Y	165ºF for 15 seconds	Reheating log	Hot - Reheat to 165 ºF for 15 sec. if temp. is < 135 ºF and was > 135 ºF or higher within the last 2 hours. Cold - Discard food if can't determine how long the food temp. was >41 ºF.	(who) review logs or training records	
HOLD		Y	Hot 135ºF or higher Cold 41ºF or below	Temperature logs		(who) review logs weekly	
SERVE		Y ###	Proper handwashing No bare hand contact Cleaning/sanitizing Exclusion of ill staff	Observation	Retain employees	Observation (who) review incident logs or training records	
PREREQUISITE PROGRAMS			SOPs: Handwashing, Thawing, No Bare Hand contact with RTE, FIFO, etc... Approved source; etc...				

This could be an example of where your receiving SOP is used and that receiving is not a CCP. This will depend on the way you run your operation.
Things like handwashing, cleaning and sanitizing SOP's would also apply.

Process 1: Food Preparation with No Cook Step

Menu Items/Products				
Example Products	Beef (item)	Chicken	Fish	Other
Example Biological Hazards	*Salmonella*	*Salmonella*	*Salmonella*	
	*E. coli*O157:H7	*Campylobacter*	*Anisakis Simplex*	
	Clostridium perfringens	*Clostridium perfringens*	*Vibrio*	
	Bacillus cereus	*Bacillus cereus*		
	Various fecal-oral route pathogens	Various fecal-oral route pathogens	Various fecal-oral route pathogens	
Example Control Measures (there may be others) CCPs & CLs	**Refrigeration** 41 °F or below	**Refrigeration** 41 °F or below	**Refrigeration** 41 °F or below	
	No bare hand contact with RTE food, proper handwashing, exclusion/ restriction of ill employees	No bare hand contact with RTE food, proper handwashing, exclusion/ restriction of ill employees	No bare hand contact with RTE food, proper handwashing, exclusion/ restriction of ill employees	
Example Monitoring	Temp product upon receipt	Temp product upon receipt	Temp product upon receipt	
	Temp check of holding facility every 4 hrs.	Temp check of holding facility every 4 hrs.	Temp check of holding facility every 4 hrs.	
	Complete appropriate log sheet	Complete appropriate log sheet	Complete appropriate log sheet	
	Observe proper handwashing practices	Observe proper handwashing practices	Observe proper handwashing practices	
Example Corrective Actions	Rapid chill to 41 °F	Rapid chill to 41 °F	Rapid chill to 41 °F	
	Re-train and enforce proper handwashing technique	Re-train and enforce proper handwashing technique	Re-train and enforce proper handwashing technique	
Example Verification	Observe the Temperature taking procedures	Observe the Temperature taking procedures	Observe the Temperature taking procedures	
	Confirm that equipment is working properly	Confirm that equipment is working properly	Confirm that equipment is working properly	
	Check temp logs for product and equipment	Check temp logs for product and equipment	Check temp logs for product and equipment	
	Verification Forms	Verification Forms	Verification Forms	
	Review Monitoring Records	Review Monitoring Records	Review Monitoring Records	
Example Records	Product Temp Logs	Product Temp Logs	Product Temp Logs	
	Equipment Temp Logs	Equipment Temp Logs	Equipment Temp Logs	
	Monitoring Records	Monitoring Records	Monitoring Records	
	Verification Records	Verification Records	Verification Records	

Process 1: Food Preparation with No Cook Step

Menu Items/Products				
Example Products	Eggs	Dairy	**Sliced Sandwich Meats/ Deli Meats**	Other
Example Biological Hazards	Salmonella	Salmonella	Listeria	
		Listeria	Staphylococcus Aureus	
		Campylobacter		
		E. coliO157:H7		
	Various fecal-oral route pathogens	Various fecal-oral route pathogens		
Example Control Measures (there may be others) CCPs & CLs	**Refrigeration** 41 °F or below	**Refrigeration** 41 °F or below	**Refrigeration** 41 °F or below	
	No bare hand contact with RTE food, proper handwashing, exclusion/ restriction of ill employees	No bare hand contact with RTE food, proper handwashing, exclusion/ restriction of ill employees	No bare hand contact with RTE food, proper handwashing, exclusion/ restriction of ill employees	
Example Monitoring	Temp product upon receipt	Temp product upon receipt	Temp product upon receipt	
	Temp check of holding facility every 4 hrs.	Temp check of holding facility every 4 hrs.	Temp check of holding facility every 4 hrs.	
	Complete appropriate log sheet	Complete appropriate log sheet	Complete appropriate log sheet	
	Observe proper handwashing practices	Observe proper handwashing practices	Observe proper handwashing practices	
Example Corrective Actions	Rapid chill to 41 °F	Rapid chill to 41 °F	Rapid chill to 41 °F	
	Re-train and enforce proper handwashing technique	Re-train and enforce proper handwashing technique	Re-train and enforce proper handwashing technique	
Example Verification	Observe the Temperature taking procedures	Observe the Temperature taking procedures	Observe the Temperature taking procedures	
	Confirm that equipment is working properly	Confirm that equipment is working properly	Confirm that equipment is working properly	
	Check temp logs for product and equipment	Check temp logs for product and equipment	Check temp logs for product and equipment	
	Verification Forms	Verification Forms	Verification Forms	
	Review Monitoring Records	Review Monitoring Records	Review Monitoring Records	
Example Records	Product Temp Logs	Product Temp Logs	Product Temp Logs	
	Equipment Temp Logs	Product Temp Logs	Product Temp Logs	
	Monitoring Records	Monitoring Records	Monitoring Records	
	Verification Records	Verification Records	Verification Records	

HACCP Implementation – a Quick Reference Manual

Process 2: Preparation for Same Day Service

Menu Items/Products

	Beef (item)	Chicken	Fish	Other
Example Products	Beef (item)	Chicken	Fish	Other
Example Biological Hazards	*Salmonella*	*Salmonella*	*Salmonella*	
	E. coli O157:H7	*Campylobacter*	*Anisakis Simplex*	
	Clostridium perfringens	*Clostridium perfringens*	*Vibrio*	
	Bacillus cereus	*Bacillus cereus*		
	Various fecal-oral route pathogens	Various fecal-oral route pathogens	Various fecal-oral route pathogens	
Example Control Measures (there may be others) CCPs & CLs	**Cooking at 155 °F for 15 seconds**	**Cooking at 165 °F for 15 seconds**	**Cooking at 145 °F for 15 seconds**	
	Refrigeration 41 °F or below	**Refrigeration** 41 °F or below	**Refrigeration** 41 °F or below	
	Hot Holding at 135 °F or above OR Time Control for 4 hours or less	**Hot Holding** at 135 °F or above OR Time Control for 4 hours or less	**Hot Holding** at 135 °F or above OR Time Control for 4 hours or less	
	No bare hand contact with RTE food, proper handwashing, exclusion/ restriction of ill employees	No bare hand contact with RTE food, proper handwashing, exclusion/ restriction of ill employees	No bare hand contact with RTE food, proper handwashing, exclusion/ restriction of ill employees	
Example Monitoring	Check Temp on finish of cooking Process **155 °F, 15 sec**	Check Temp on finish of cooking Process **165 °F, 15 sec**	Check Temp on finish of cooking Process **145 °F, 15 sec**	
	Temp food in Cold Holding step 41 °F	Temp food in Cold Holding step 41 °F	Temp food in Cold Holding step 41 °F	
	Temp Hot holding-135 °F or Above	Temp Hot holding-135 °F or Above	Temp Hot holding-135 °F or Above	
	Observe proper hand washing and final service method	Observe proper hand washing and final service method	Observe proper hand washing and final service method	
Example Corrective Actions	Continue cooking until correct internal temperature is reached	Continue cooking until correct internal temperature is reached	Continue cooking until correct internal temperature is reached	
	Rapid chill to 41 °F	Rapid chill to 41 °F	Rapid chill to 41 °F	
	Re-Therm Product if necessary-reset or repair hot-holding equipment	Re-Therm Product if necessary-reset or repair hot-holding equipment	Re-Therm Product if necessary-reset or repair hot-holding equipment	
	Re-train and enforce proper handwashing technique	Re-train and enforce proper handwashing technique	Re-train and enforce proper handwashing technique	
Example Verification	Observe the Temperature taking procedures	Observe the Temperature taking procedures	Observe the Temperature taking procedures	
	Confirm that equipment is working properly	Confirm that equipment is working properly	Confirm that equipment is working properly	
	Check temp logs for product and equipment	Check temp logs for product and equipment	Check temp logs for product and equipment	
	Verification Forms	Verification Forms	Verification Forms	
	Review Monitoring Records	Review Monitoring Records	Review Monitoring Records	
Example Records	Product Temp Logs	Product Temp Logs	Product Temp Logs	
	Equipment Temp Logs	Equipment Temp Logs	Equipment Temp Logs	
	Monitoring Records	Monitoring Records	Monitoring Records	
	Verification Records	Verification Records	Verification Records	

Process 2: Preparation for Same Day Service

Menu Items/Products				
Example Products	Eggs	Dairy	**Starchy Foods-rice, Potatoes**	Other
Example Biological Hazards	*Salmonella*	*Salmonella*	*Bacillus Cereus*	
	Various fecal-oral route pathogens	Various fecal-oral route pathogens	Various fecal-oral route pathogens	
Example Control Measures (there may be others) CCPs & CLs	**Cooking at 145 °F for 15 seconds**			
	Refrigeration 41 °F or below	**Refrigeration** 41 °F or below	**Refrigeration** 41 °F or below	
	Hot Holding at 135 °F or above OR Time Control for 4 hours or less		**Hot Holding** at 135 °F or above OR Time Control for 4 hours or less	
	No bare hand contact with RTE food, proper handwashing, exclusion/ restriction of ill employees	No bare hand contact with RTE food, proper handwashing, exclusion/ restriction of ill employees	No bare hand contact with RTE food, proper handwashing, exclusion/ restriction of ill employees	
Example Monitoring	Check Temp on finish of cooking Process **145 °F, 15 sec**		Check Temp on finish of cooking Process **145 °F, 15 sec**	
	Temp food in Cold Holding step 41 °F	Temp food in Cold Holding step 41 °F	Temp food in Cold Holding step 41 °F	
	Temp Hot holding-135 °F or Above		Temp Hot holding-135 °F or Above	
	Observe proper hand washing and final service method	Observe proper hand washing and final service method	Observe proper hand washing and final service method	
Example Corrective Actions	Continue cooking until correct internal temperature is reached		Continue cooking until correct internal temperature is reached	
	Rapid chill to 41 °F	Rapid chill to 41 °F	Rapid chill to 41 °F	
	Re-Therm Product if necessary-reset or repair hot-holding equipment		Re-Therm Product if necessary-reset or repair hot-holding equipment	
	Re-train and enforce proper handwashing technique	Re-train and enforce proper handwashing technique	Re-train and enforce proper handwashing technique	
Example Verification	Observe the Temperature taking procedures	Observe the Temperature taking procedures	Observe the Temperature taking procedures	
	Confirm that equipment is working properly	Confirm that equipment is working properly	Confirm that equipment is working properly	
	Check temp logs for product and equipment	Check temp logs for product and equipment	Check temp logs for product and equipment	
	Verification Forms	Verification Forms	Verification Forms	
	Review Monitoring Records	Review Monitoring Records	Review Monitoring Records	
Example Records	Product Temp Logs	Product Temp Logs	Product Temp Logs	
	Equipment Temp Logs	Equipment Temp Logs	Equipment Temp Logs	
	Monitoring Records	Monitoring Records	Monitoring Records	
	Verification Records	Verification Records	Verification Records	

Process 3: Complex Food Preparation

Menu Items/Products				
Example Products	Beef (item)	Chicken	Gravies	Other
Example Biological Hazards	*Salmonella*	*Salmonella*	*Salmonella*	
	*E. coli*O157:H7	*Campylobacter*	*Campylobacter*	
	Clostridium perfringens	*Clostridium perfringens*	*Clostridium perfringens*	
	Bacillus cereus	*Bacillus cereus*	*Bacillus cereus*	
	Various fecal-oral route pathogens	Various fecal-oral route pathogens	Various fecal-oral route pathogens	
Example Control Measures (there may be others) CCPs & CLs	**Cooking at 155 °F for 15 seconds**	**Cooking at 165 °F for 15 seconds**	**Cooking at 165 °F for 15 seconds**	
	Cool to 135°F to 70°F within 2 hrs. & 70°F to 41°F within 4 hrs.	**Cool** to 135°F to 70°F within 2 hrs. & 70°F to 41°F within 4 hrs.	**Cool** to 135°F to 70°F within 2 hrs. & 70°F to 41°F within 4 hrs.	
	Re-heat to 165 °F for 15 seconds	**Re-heat to 165 °F for 15 seconds**	**Re-heat to 165 °F for 15 seconds**	
	Hot Holding at 135 °F or above OR Time Control for 4 hours or less	**Hot Holding** at 135 °F or above OR Time Control for 4 hours or less	**Hot Holding** at 135 °F or above OR Time Control for 4 hours or less	
	No bare hand contact with RTE food, proper handwashing, exclusion/ restriction of ill employees	No bare hand contact with RTE food, proper handwashing, exclusion/ restriction of ill employees	No bare hand contact with RTE food, proper handwashing, exclusion/ restriction of ill employees	
Example Monitoring	Cooking Temp. log @ 30 min. & 1 hr.	Cooking Temp. log @ 30 min. & 1 hr.	Cooking Temp. log @ 30 min. & 1 hr.	
	Cooling Temp. log @ 2/4/6 hr. intervals	Cooling Temp. log @ 2/4/6 hr. intervals	Cooling Temp. log @ 2/4/6 hr. intervals	
	Reheating log	Reheating log	Reheating log	
	Temperature logs	Temperature logs	Temperature logs	
	Observation	Observation	Observation	
Example Corrective Actions	Continue cooking until required internal temp. is reached.	Continue cooking until required internal temp. is reached.	Continue cooking until required internal temp. is reached.	
	Discard cooked, hot food immediately when the food is: > 70 °F and > 2 hours into the cooling process	Discard cooked, hot food immediately when the food is: > 70 °F and > 2 hours into the cooling process	Discard cooked, hot food immediately when the food is: > 70 °F and > 2 hours into the cooling process	
	Reheat to 165 °F for 15 sec. if temp. is <135 °F and was >135 °F or higher within the last 2 hours.	Reheat to 165 °F for 15 sec. Is temp. Is <135 °F and was >135 °F or higher within the last 2 hours.	Reheat to 165 °F for 15 sec. if temp. is <135 °F and was >135 °F or higher within the last 2 hours.	
	Discard food if can't determine how long the food temp. was >41 °F.	Discard food if can't determine how long the food temp. was >41 °F.	Discard food if can't determine how long the food temp. was >41 °F.	
	Continue cooking until required internal temp. is reached.	Continue cooking until required internal temp. is reached.	Continue cooking until required internal temp. is reached.	
	Re-train and enforce proper handwashing technique	Re-train and enforce proper handwashing technique	Re-train and enforce proper handwashing technique	
Example Verification	Designated HACCP Team member will: Review receiving logs monthly. Temp. logs weekly Thermometer calibration log weekly Etc…			
Example Records	Vendor Guarantees Food Safety Checklist Thermometer calibration log Quarterly, semi-annual & yearly audit sheets		SOPs Manager Checklist Temperature logs Etc…	